How to
HAVE A KID
and a Life

How to
HAVE A KID
and a Life

A Survival Guide

ERICKA SÓUTER

sounds true
BOULDER, COLORADO

Sounds True
Boulder, CO 80306

Published 2021

Cover design by Jenny Miles
Book design by Meredith March

The wood used to produce this book is from
Forest Stewardship Council (FSC) certified forests,
recycled materials, or controlled wood.

Printed in the United States of America

Library of Congress Cataloging-in-Publication Data
Names: Sóuter, Ericka, author.
Title: How to Have a Kid and a Life: A Survival Guide / Ericka Sóuter.
Description: Boulder, CO : Sounds True, 2021. | Includes bibliographical
   references.
Identifiers: LCCN 2020045888 (print) | LCCN 2020045889 (ebook) |
   ISBN 9781683644873 (paperback) | ISBN 9781683644880 (ebook)
Subjects: LCSH: Motherhood. | Working mothers. | Work-life balance.
Classification: LCC HQ759 .S6456 2021 (print) | LCC HQ759 (ebook) |
   DDC 306.874/3–dc23
LC record available at https://lccn.loc.gov/2020045888
LC ebook record available at https://lccn.loc.gov/2020045889

10 9 8 7 6 5 4 3 2 1

To Caleb:
The most loving, supportive, and patient
husband a person can have.

To Lex and Aidan:
Being your mom has changed me in ways I never
imagined. It's a privilege to love you, care for
you, and have lightsaber battles with you.

*To my mother Anita, grandmother Ethel,
and aunts Debbie, Nancy, and Annie:*
Thank you for teaching me how to be a strong,
determined, resilient, and loving woman.

CONTENTS

Nine

Ten

Eleven

Introduction

A Reintroduction to Motherhood: The Baby Isn't the Only Newborn in Your House

I don't think I have the mom gene," I used to tell friends with a laugh after a particularly tough day of being chauffeur, chef, hairstylist, laundress, maid, boo-boo healer, referee, mediator, homework helper, birthday organizer, and everything else motherhood entails. While I passed it off as a joke, I really did wonder if I was cut out for this. Was it *this* hard for everyone? Other women seemed so much more together. I couldn't figure out how to manage it all—work, marriage, kids, breathing room. I felt lost. So when I came across research suggesting that there was an actual mom gene, I became obsessed with the idea. Then an editor at CafeMom, I wrote an essay asking if the discovery of a mom gene could be the reason some of us find motherhood so hard. Could it be that some of us are better at it because of biology? It really resonated with readers. So many had been struggling. Many more than I realized. It sparked conversations, not just about being maternal but also about all the other unspoken challenges of motherhood. That is when I knew I wanted to write this book.

Like so many first-time moms, I was under the naïve impression that living with a newborn would be the hardest adjustment to parenthood. After all, as soon as you announce that you are expecting, everyone who has ever been within five feet of a baby bombards you with warnings about sleep schedules, colic, and my personal fave, never being able to pee in peace again. It's all well-meaning, of course, but it's far from the complete truth. In those first several months, you will learn that the turbulence of life with a baby is not actually the toughest part of your newly minted mommy status.

I have had the great fortune to spend hundreds of hours talking to mothers across the country from different racial, ethnic, religious, and socioeconomic backgrounds. Some longed to be moms their entire lives. Others debated whether it was something they wanted up until the day they found themselves staring at those two lines on a pregnancy test. No matter their path to parenthood, they all shared one universal truth: what they desperately wanted and could not find were real, meaningful discussions about the confidence-shaking, anxiety-causing, what-the-hell-happened-to-me, and why-doesn't-anyone-see-me-anymore reality of becoming a mother.

Before our blessed bundles arrive, our lives are filled with complications from work, romance, friendships, self-image, and much more. These issues become even more complex once kids are in the picture. New moms deal with everything from a sudden friction in their marriages to grown-up mean girls to navigating full-time careers alongside more-than-full-time motherhood. Perhaps Adrienne Rich captured it best in *Of Woman Born*:

No one mentions that psychic crisis of bearing a first child, the excitation of long-buried feelings about one's own mother, the sense of confused power and powerlessness, or being taken over on the one hand and of touching new physical and psychic potentialities on the other, a heightened sensibility which can be exhilarating, bewildering and exhausting.[1]

It's enough to push you to the brink, but I'm here to tell you it doesn't have to. We just need to change the way we think and talk about motherhood. You see, when you become a mom, you are not just giving birth to a baby. A new you emerges as well. And it can feel like a seismic change. In fact, back in 1973 medical anthropologist Dana Raphael (who coined the term *doula*) named this life shift *matrescence*. Sounds like *adolescence*, and that's not by accident. According to Raphael, matrescence is like experiencing puberty all over again.

I turned to Dr. Aurélie Athan, a reproductive psychologist and Columbia University professor who has dedicated her life's work to this subject, for a deeper understanding. She was looking at the psychology of women over a life span, which meant taking a look at how life-welcoming events like having a child affect us. "Women were telling me about the good, the bad, the ugly, and the beautiful," she effused. "And they were telling me a lot about growth experiences, in the way they were stretched and deepened. They were telling me this was the most crippling and rewarding experience, both at the same time." It was apparent that motherhood was two sides of the same coin. One superb, one savage.

We have been conditioned to think a woman becomes a mother as soon as she gives birth. Of course, that's biologically true, but it's nowhere near as simple as that. Shifting from autonomous human to mom is more akin to a journey rather than one signifying event. And like puberty, it can be awkward, ugly, and uncomfortable. Your body changes, you get pimples and stretch marks. You are moody, emotional, and easily irritated. It even mimics the relationships of adolescence in the sense that social dynamics change, people drop out of your life, and loyalties realign. Sounds fun, right? Don't worry, you will survive. In fact, you will love it if you know what to expect.

This transition to motherhood is different for every woman, according to Dr. Athan. In that sense, there is no exact beginning and no exact end point. The start for each of us is what she calls the "oh shit moment." It's the point when motherhood becomes real for you. For some, it could be the moment that all ten of those pregnancy tests you've peed on say positive or the first time you feel those quickening flutters in your pregnant belly. For Connecticut mom of two Natalie, it happened the second after her first baby was born. "I felt for the first time in my life I was in the right place," gushed the writer, who blogs about motherhood and mental health at NatsNextAdventure.com. "It felt so peaceful. I was her mom." That feeling doesn't always happen right away. It didn't hit Tomika, a single mom from Virginia, until weeks after her son was placed in her arms. Her parents had been with her in the beginning, and this helped smooth the start of motherhood, but when they left, it dawned on her that this was real. Her life would never be the same. She and only she was responsible for this baby's survival.

What follows for each of us is a roller coaster in the truest sense. There are times you will be fraught but then rebound only to find yourself completely crazed again. This is the reason we can feel so much disorientation in those early days. And this process gets reawakened with every child and at every developmental stage because mothering a newborn requires a different set of skills than dealing with a preteen or a young adult. We are constantly evolving, learning, and getting little shell shocks along the way. When I explain the concept of matrescence to moms, the first question is usually, "How do I avoid it?" Sorry. No escaping this one, but being aware of what's ahead will make you feel a lot less crazy. Trust me.

One of the most common ways we respond to the ups and downs of motherhood is by giving more of ourselves— more time, more attention, more involvement, more, more, and more. Many of us forego our own passions and interests, our own friends, our own lives. And this, we are told, is the way it's supposed to be. Even for those of us who return to work outside the home.

When we do appear to be coming apart at the seams, those around us love to encourage "me time," as if a thirty-minute mani-pedi or SoulCycle class is the cure for what ails us. The truth is, the requirements of modern motherhood can leave us feeling swallowed up whole, wondering, *Where did I go?* It's fair to say that we are all well aware that motherhood will be hard. We just didn't realize it would be *this* hard. The important question to ask is, What are we going to do about it? How do we move past talking or complaining and make meaningful change in our own lives?

I do think it's possible to ease the transition to motherhood by truly understanding the changes that can and will occur in every aspect of our lives. And I don't mean remedying that yucky cradle cap peeling off your baby's scalp or the horrors of potty-training a three-year-old (the nightmare I am enduring as I write this). So much about our world becomes gnarled, from our sex lives to career paths and even our relationships with other women.

Why aren't we talking about that?

If we start looking at motherhood as a time of change and development for us too, perhaps moms can start getting the care and attention they need as well. Think of it this way: when there is a speed bump ahead in the road, you adjust your speed so you can maneuver it more smoothly. Why can't we prep for the pitfalls of parent life the same way? My greatest hope is that this short tome helps make that possible. I hope it teaches you three things:

1. It's high time we all got authentic about what mothers go through beyond the day-to-day rigors of childcare.

2. Not loving every minute of family time does not make you a terrible person. Yes, this may be something you dreamed of and planned for, but real life brims with as many moments of joy as frustration.

You have the right to feel however you feel about it, and you don't need to apologize for that.

3. Though going forward you will forever be known as so-and-so's mom, your existence is not defined only by the fact you have children. There will inevitably be a tug-of-war between our family's needs and our own. It's okay to win some of those rounds. Our happiness matters too.

One

The Myth of Modern Motherhood

WHAT TO REALLY EXPECT:
When you sacrifice everything for your
children, you may be sacrificing
your own happiness in the process.

When I first met Amanda, she was one week into motherhood, sitting in the middle of her living room floor surrounded by three huge foam tires, a bonnet that looked more like a swatch of designer Teflon, an indestructible steel frame, and what the instruction booklet called a brushed aluminum chassis, "Whatever the hell that is," she said, rolling her eyes. These were all parts of the overpriced, all-terrain stroller that, as so many web posts promised, would make outdoor walks with her baby a breeze. Though up to that very moment, it had only managed to leave her on the verge of tears.

As she stared at components that looked more like car parts than the makings of a must-have baby accessory, she couldn't help but think about all those other smiling moms she'd seen tooling about Manhattan with babies in Bugaboos. By comparison, she didn't know how she was going to even make it out the door, much less through the next eighteen years. She read all the books and blogs, bought all the right stuff, but she felt like a disaster.

"I'm a hot mess," she confessed, hair sweat-soaked and heart pounding as her daughter wailed in the nursery a few feet away.

But even after she managed to assemble the stroller, an overwhelming unease lingered for weeks, then months, and then years. "Going into all this, I wasn't delusional about motherhood, I knew it would be hard," she conceded. Amanda understood that "having it all" was a load of bull, unless you could somehow defy the space-time continuum. The one thing she didn't expect was to sacrifice so much of what she loved about the life she had spent the previous three decades building. "One day I'm a career woman moving up the ladder, and the next I feel like I'm drowning taking care of a baby, keeping the house from looking like a total wreck, cooking dinner, and somehow figuring how to still kick ass at work," she thoughtfully lamented. "It's like I'm constantly treading water with land nowhere in sight."

The Happiness Gap

It's a frightfully common refrain among women the world over. A study of twenty-two countries reported that parents in the United States tend to be unhappier than nonparents.[1] The researchers call this the parenting happiness gap, and American parents proved to be the most miserable. The reasons are manifold. Yes, kids bring an undeniable amount of joy to our lives—and the respondents said as much. But they are also exhausting and expensive, and US parents have the added pressure of dealing with poor maternity/paternity, vacation, and sick leave policies; unsubsidized childcare; and very little work flexibility. Among the hundreds of mothers I interviewed, most admit the problem is in the chasm between what they thought parenthood would be like and what it is like in reality. It's a basic issue of expectation versus stark reality.

No matter how much you read about parenthood or how often you watch your friends juggling life, work, and kids, you can't possibly prepare for what it's going to feel like *to you*.

On top of that, there is the unrelenting social pressure that makes motherhood so punishing. The Pew Research Center released findings showing that women face more pressure than men to be involved parents and more than one-third fear they don't give their kids enough attention.[2] "You are expected to take care of the kids, pick up your career without missing a beat, take care of the house, and have sex with your husband," explained professor Elizabeth Velez, a lecturer in the Women's and Gender Studies program at Georgetown University. "Meeting all those expectations is impossible."

An Epidemic of Mommy Malaise

By her own estimation, Amanda wasn't doing anything well—not mothering, not marriage, and certainly not work. Somehow taking care of her children and carving out time to focus on herself were incompatible goals. When she did do something "selfish," like take a work-related seminar on the weekend, she felt guilty, and that guilt plagued her. Though perhaps more dismaying is the fact that she had resigned herself to believing that this is how motherhood is supposed to be. How it has to be.

"It's not about us, right?" she asked rhetorically.

It's a comment I've heard countless times. That is the way we've been taught to think about parenthood. Children come into this world vulnerable and needy, so naturally they should be our top priority. At the same time that women have been pressing for social and economic parity with men, the fundamental parenting duties still fall on us. And somewhere along the line, being an attentive, good parent became synonymous with giving up all the other things that were important in our lives. It meant sacrificing everything that made you, you.

As time ticked on, Amanda focused less and less on the goals and hopes for herself she had long held. She felt as though each year she lost more of what made her special and unique. This feeling of losing her core identity made her unhappy, and the guilt about feeling unhappy made her even more depressed. She wasn't alone. This mommy malaise has become the rule rather than the exception. A 2015 German study found that being a parent actually creates more unhappiness than divorce, unemployment, or even the death of a spouse.[3] This cannot be the way mothers are meant to exist in this society.

How Did We Get Here?

Of course, our own moms are our first exposure to how a woman is supposed to function in this world. When I asked women to share memories of their mothers, the initial descriptions were always a mix of adoration and reverence. They used words like *selfless, dedicated, wise, hardworking, beautiful, strong,* and *inspiring.* The list of glowing adjectives was endless. When pressed to go deeper, to consider what life was like *for* Mom, rather than merely *with* her, the narrative changed drastically.

"My mom was always tired."

"It was hard for her taking care of all of us."

"We drove her crazy."

"She had to raise us all by herself. She struggled."

"My mom never really did anything just for herself. It was always about us."

"I was mad when she went back to school. I wanted her home. I made her feel guilty."

"Four kids under five! She had to be overwhelmed."

"I don't really remember her ever doing anything for herself."

It's sobering to realize that we subconsciously learned at such an early age that becoming mothers means stifling our most basic wants and needs.

The media also influences how we parent. "[Media] has the power to shape our thinking," notes Rachel Rubin, PhD, professor of American Studies at the University of Massachusetts. "Those images help define our expectations of what it's like to be a mom in America." A "good mother" has long been defined in our culture as self-sacrificing, unwaveringly generous, and forever putting her family's needs before her own (not that she has any). This image can be traced back as early as the 1800s when women, especially white women, were heralded for their supposed one true purpose: to procreate and cater to a husband. Lydia Maria Child, a noted abolitionist, Native American rights activist, journalist, and women's rights activist was considered quite progressive for her time, yet still promoted the notion that a woman's primary role was to tend to home and family. In her once-celebrated *The Mother's Book*, she gave instruction on the proper way to show affection to a child, how to teach a daughter to find a good husband, and the virtues of a good woman.

"A knowledge of domestic duties is beyond all price to a woman," wrote Child, who would have been considered an early nineteenth-century influencer, if there were such a thing back then. "Everyone ought to know how to sew, and knit, and mend, and cook, and superintend a household. In every situation of life, high or low, this sort of knowledge is a great advantage. There is no necessity that the gaining of such information should interfere with intellectual acquirements, or even with elegant accomplishments. A well-regulated mind can find time to attend to all."[4]

By the 1950s, television showed us the ideal in black-and-white. These women, again largely Caucasian, vacuumed in pearls and heels; had warm, delicious dinners on the table every evening; and always did so with a cherry-red lipstick-laced smile. Shows like *Donna Reed*,

Leave It to Beaver, *Father Knows Best*, and *The Adventures of Ozzie & Harriet* depicted the ever-contented "happy housewife." Sweet, nurturing, patient, undemanding, and gives love unconditionally. "In these shows, women were pictured in the living room and kitchen and almost never outside the home," said Velez, who teaches a course that looks at false representations of motherhood. Perhaps most confounding was the fact the house was always spotless and uncluttered. "These shows reflected a reality that was desired," she continued. "The fathers in these shows had been to war, come back, and now laid down the law." This was the American Dream—or so we were supposed to think it was—because everyone always seemed happy and complete. Though, we know how shamefully incomplete this depiction actually was. African American and Latina women were hardly vacuuming in pearls. Let's be honest, most women, regardless of race or socioeconomic group, weren't doing housework in heels.

What about the single mom? What about the working mom? It's as though women with physical limitations didn't exist. And never mind the grandmothers and aunts who took up the mantle of mother when there was no other choice. Anything other than this idealized, Norman Rockwell image of family and motherhood was largely, if not wholly, ignored in popular culture.

If the '50s were the era of lamblike submission, the '60s thankfully gave women a bold new voice. Betty Friedan's *The Feminine Mystique* challenged the belief that being a housewife and mother was the prescription for happiness. She surveyed suburban women across the country and analyzed how magazines, advertisers, and even the education system created a narrow definition of what their lives should be like.

> The problem lay buried, unspoken, for many years in the minds of American women. It was a strange stirring, a sense of dissatisfaction, a yearning that women suffered in the middle of the twentieth century in the United States. Each suburban wife struggles with it alone. As she made the beds, shopped for groceries, matched slipcover material, ate peanut butter sandwiches with her children, chauffeured Cub Scouts and Brownies, lay beside her husband at night—she was afraid to ask even of herself the silent question—"Is this all?"[5]

I love to think how shocking it was for people of the time to read this unapologetic skewering of the status quo. Friedan was a woman ahead of her time, calling this circumstance that confined so many women the "problem that has no name." Over the next fifty years, female television and film characters evolved to be more independent and savvier, often having interests beyond their families. An Enjoli perfume commercial claimed we could "bring home the bacon. Fry it up in a pan. And never let him forget he's a man!" These were noteworthy strides, but despite the changes in what a "good mom" could do or what she looked like, her purpose remained the same: happily take care of her family without complaint or an ounce of regret.

By the 1980s, the dutiful housewife was a remnant of the past, and the era of the supermom emerged. Ads for the cigarette brand Virginia Slims proclaimed, "You've come a long way, baby." Women had more opportunities and were more independent than ever, and still the good mom template dominated. *Growing Pains, Family Ties,* and *The Cosby Show* depicted high-power career women who also managed to maintain spotless homes, happy marriages, and enviably close relationships with their children. Attorney Clair Huxtable, journalist Maggie Seaver, and architect Elyse Keaton were most frequently mentioned as the favorite TV moms among both women and men I polled. They were emblematic of many ideals: they were always impeccably dressed and gave the kids great advice, which the kids actually listened to. These characters had it all and made us believe we could too. However, lost in our adoration was the fact that they still carried the burden of gender-assigned jobs, like cooking, cleaning, and being the primary nurturer on top of trying to maintain kick-ass careers. You don't need a degree to know that this is much easier to pull off on TV than in real life.

Shows like *Modern Family* and *Black-ish* bring much needed diversity to the small screen definition of family life, challenging that "normal" image of white, gendered parenting. "But for the most part, we still see happy families that take on traditional roles," Professor Velez broke it down. "In *Modern Family*, within the gay couple one is more feminine and the primary caretaker of their child. While the culture has changed, our expectations of mothers have not. When it comes to real-world parenthood, it's the same old standards. It's still all on mom. It's still supposed to be the only thing she wants and needs." Even in this day and age, portrayals of moms continue to fall short. Professor Rubin noted that there is still a class-based model of motherhood at play with working-class or impoverished families underrepresented in the media landscape. Motherhood comes off as a lifestyle choice rather than a true reflection of our realities. It's misleading and creates unrealistic expectations for us.

TV and film also tend to portray an oversimplified version of family life with every issue being resolved by the time the credits roll. The first half of the motion picture *Tully* depicts a harsh truth: motherhood can suck—hard. The main character, Marlo, is plagued by exhaustion from the constant drumbeat of baby care, housework, and raising two older children, one of whom is autistic. Her husband is kind but clueless as he criticizes her lazy dinner choice of frozen pizza. When I saw the movie, you could hear many exasperated "been there" sighs in the theater during that particular scene.

"The first half tells the truth of motherhood, but the story is wrapped up too neatly," observed Velez. "Turns out she has postpartum depression, she takes medicine, and everything is fine now. In real life, you are going to continue dealing with this stuff. It's not wrapped up in a neat bow. It sends the wrong message."

Stars Are *Not* Just Like Us

Celebrity moms have also set an impractical standard. Magazines celebrate their perfect baby bumps and praise them for slipping back into skinny jeans weeks after giving birth. We never see bags under their eyes or greasy, unwashed hair. They brag about loving their pregnant bodies, adoring the chaos of family life, and feeling perfect even when covered in spit-up while on conference calls.

Of course it's easier to feel content with the everyday hardships of child-rearing when you have so many resources at your disposal. During my time as a magazine writer, I was once dispatched to a morning show to talk about the arrival of Jennifer Lopez's twins. Per our cover story, I was supposed to gush about how "hands-on" she was with her babies. Even as the words came out of my mouth, I knew how ridiculous it must have sounded to the typical viewer saddled at home with two kids and no help. Later, a colleague told me the segment ended up on *Talk Soup*, a show that parodied celeb news. Apparently, the comic host thought it was a silly notion too.

Do I believe Lopez changed diapers and got up for middle-of-the night feedings? Yes, I do. But did she likely have an army of nannies, assistants, chefs, and various other staff to step in at a second's notice? Absolutely. And that surely takes the edge off. Her career would never have to take a back seat to motherhood unless she wanted it to.

Even though we know the lives of celebrities are nothing like ours, we still try to emulate them on some level. Not only do we have to be great mothers, we have to be beautiful too. In our celebrity-obsessed culture, this can create an intense amount of pressure. These ideals can be so powerful that failure to live up to them can make us feel like bad moms, reports a Duke University study on mothering.[6]

That's hard to live with considering that, according to the Pew Research Center, a majority of Americans think being a parent is one of the most important parts of their identity.[7]

Unhappy People Have Unhappy Kids

There is a severe cost to accepting a life that is unsatisfying at best and downright miserable at worst. As unhappy as they may be, so many parents find solace in the fact that their kids are happy—at least they hope they are.

Amanda worried that her own children were affected by the anguish that seemed to reverberate beneath her skin—like the bass from a stereo speaker. It's a well-founded fear. Using achievement tests, teachers' descriptions of child behavior in class, and interviews, while closely looking at family relationships, Carolyn and Philip Cowan, husband and wife psychologists and professors emeritus at the University of California, Berkeley, (along with professor and psychologist Neera Mehta) found that it was possible to predict how a child will do emotionally, socially, and academically.[8] The biggest factor? How the parents are doing individually and as a couple.

Their research was inspired by their own marriage. "We were young parents and partners and young professionals trying to manage all those things," explained Carolyn. "We weren't having so much trouble with the parenting part. We have three kids. They're fairly close together, about two years apart. But we were trying to figure out what had happened to our relationship as a couple. Where did it go?"[9] That question eventually led to the creation of their landmark ten-year study that followed one hundred couples after the arrival of their first child.

The Cowans considered many factors, including an individual's anxiety and depression, how competent and confident they were, and what it was like growing up in their childhood homes and what they would like to change. When they turned the lens toward how the couple functions, they looked at stressors like work, finances, even drug and alcohol problems. Then they dissected how the pair dealt with challenges and what they do when they disagree.

They discovered that if you are not happy, your children know it. And absorb it. Of course, life happens, and we can't always control how we respond. Adults can be rattled by a myriad of causes other than their kids: career, relationships, social dynamics, and their health. And repeatedly, these were all issues moms said they put on the backburner to focus on their kids' needs. However, the Cowans found that children suffer if the people taking care of them are not taking care of themselves.

It's an unsettling realization for most parents I interviewed. No one wants to be the unwitting cause of a child's misery. It was certainly a hard truth for Lisa and her husband, John, to accept. After a year of dealing with a sullen and moody preteen, they sent him to a child psychologist. Two sessions in, the doctor made it clear that if the parents didn't deal with their own issues, their son wouldn't be happy either.

In the book *Raising Happiness: 10 Simple Steps for More Joyful Kids and Happier Parents*, Christine Carter notes extensive research showing mothers who feel depressed are more likely to have children who act out or have other behavioral problems.[10] Many experts echo this claim. Parental depression may make them less effective parents. "Unless you are addressing your suffering, your kids are taking in all of it," warned New York City-based psychotherapist Sarah McCaslin, also an ordained pastor. She often works with parents who are experiencing depression and anxiety and finds a connection between their emotional state and that of their children. Day-to-day behavior—from the way you deal with little frustrations to the tone of your voice—can potentially impact the way your child acts.

Let's consider the famous Bobo doll experiment in which researchers made sure children saw adults beating up a doll. When they were given the same doll, they imitated the behavior. "Parents rarely want to accept that they may be part of the problem, but sometimes they are," notes McCaslin. "I always ask parents how they are handling stress and pressures. Are they constantly frustrated and overwhelmed? How are they in front of their kids? Do they have support? Do they have something all their own? Where do their needs fall in the long list of priorities? It's a sobering conversation."

Researchers say that a mom's satisfaction with her life is more important to a child's social and emotional skills than how much money she has, the amount of time she spends with them, or whether she is a working or stay-at-home mom.[11] The point is, your happiness matters.

YOUR NEW TO-DO LIST

ASK YOURSELF:

1. Am I nurturing my marriage/partnership?

2. Is my career headed in a good direction (if applicable)?

3. Do I have supportive friends to turn to?

4. Do I feel good about myself?

5. Do I nurture any of the passions I had before kids?

6. Have I created a social life or hobbies that have nothing to do with my children?

If you answered no to any of these questions, it's time to reevaluate your priorities. I'm not talking about ignoring the needs of your children but rather finally tending to your own. It's a bit counterintuitive, I know. As parents, we think our sole focus should be our children. We work to take care of them; we cook to feed them; we schedule playdates and sign them up for activities to socialize them. It's what many of us experienced during our own childhoods too.

Sadly, more than fifty years since Friedan's groundbreaking work, moms still languish under a narrowly defined sphere where the "good mom" always puts her needs last. But it's way past time for that antiquated notion to evolve. The quality of your life will determine how effective and nurturing you are as a parent. During my conversations with the Cowans, one thing was crystal clear: you can have the very best of intentions, but if you are not being nurtured and supported or not feeling nurtured or supported, this will adversely affect your ability to parent the way you want to.

Being good for our kids has to become synonymous with being good to ourselves. Think of it this way: Do you want your daughters growing up to think they aren't supposed to be contented, fulfilled adults? Let's authentically model the life we want for them. Happiness for everyone in your family is a dream within reach if you are willing to put yourself back on the top of your to-do list. The chapters that follow are a guidebook for doing just that. Only by addressing the unspoken hardship of motherhood can we avoid the disillusionment that defines this epidemic of mommy malaise

Two

The Motherhood Penalty: How to Keep Your Career on Track

WHAT TO REALLY EXPECT:
If you thought you were at a disadvantage
before, that glass ceiling just got lower.

t was a journalist's dream job. I spent nine years at *People* magazine interviewing every celebrity imaginable. Oprah. Check. Drew Barrymore. Check. Matthew McConaughey. Check, check (the extra one for his abs). On the movies and music beat, I became a familiar face on the red carpet. It wasn't all glam all the time though. I enjoyed a balance, covering both the A-list stars and more altruistic topics. At a time before 24-7 access to the minutia of every person's life, my stories on exercise bulimia, plastic surgery nightmares, and the Lost Boys of the Sudan were eye-opening reads. I will never forget my Erin Brockovich moment, slogging through a murky, snake-filled creek in Franklin, Tennessee, to uncover an environmental racism conspiracy. But, as the saying goes, nothing is perfect.

Just like every other company in America, at *People*, there were office politics at play, and to my detriment, I was never very good at playing that game. I would sit in meetings marveling at how easily fellow reporters could feign genuine laughter at some editor's joke, no matter how banal or borderline offensive. And the job itself could be a little monotonous, listening to actors spew the same old cheesy anecdotes every time they had a movie to promote. As I sat across from one drool-worthy Oscar winner, I couldn't help but furrow my brow and think, *This dude told me this exact same story a year and a half ago.*

Plus, they were masterful fibbers. I was with one huge singer-actress who wouldn't stop gushing about her husband and their "fantastic" relationship. I wrote all about her great marriage for the magazine, and two weeks later she filed for divorce. Then there were those constant "body after baby" stories we had to do after every Hollywood birth. Stars always credited their *ah-maaaze-ing* trainer for helping them drop the weight fast. The real story was they just didn't eat, at least not like us mere mortals. "I don't like the taste of carbs," one actress told me with a straight face. No carbs? Not one? Really. Cue the eye roll. One slightly sadistic colleague always scheduled lunch interviews with stars just to see if they would actually put a bite of food in their mouths or just pick at the plate.

Still, for the most part, I enjoyed the work. It defined me. So much so that I put work before everything, including starting a family. There was never a good time to have a baby. Spring meant gearing up for the World's Most

Beautiful issue. Fall meant Sexiest Man Alive. Winter was awards season. I was finally working under a powerful, brilliant editor who treated her writers with kindness and respect and gave us credit for our ideas. Anyone in publishing (or any industry for that matter) knows that is like finding a unicorn. *The Devil Wears Prada* may have been a novel, but it was far from complete fiction.

There were higher-ups who treated their people like garbage. A particularly meek editorial assistant used to find refuge in my office every time her boss tormented her—which was almost daily. On an otherwise unremarkable workday, she ran in, tears streaming down her cheeks, scared because she said the editor had threatened to fire her because the milk in the coffee she dutifully fetched from his favorite café tasted "off." After listening to horror stories like that, why would I want to leave what I had come to consider a professional Camelot? And, truth be told, for years I feared having a baby would set my career back in some way. Can you sense the self-fulfilling prophecy coming?

His Biological Clock

Three years into marriage, I couldn't put it off any longer. My husband kept nagging that his biological clock was ticking (unusual gender role reversal, I know), and my incredibly traditional Cuban in-laws feared I couldn't bear a child. Though I was still ambivalent on the issue, I didn't really have a good excuse to wait any longer. My career was in a good place. My marriage was solid. A baby made sense.

Now let's fast-forward a year and a half to what started as a typical day of my maternity leave. The hectic yet tedious routine began after those first early morning cries. I was bone-tired, though my exhaustion was just as much mental as it was physical. I craved interaction with the non-mommy world.

As I lay in bed waiting for the cries to grow in intensity, I prayed this would be the day Lex would actually fall back to sleep. Wishful thinking. Delusional even. I dragged myself out from under the covers to start the diapering-feed-play-nap loop that would frame our entire day. Lex and I were somewhere in the middle of that cycle when the phone rang. I recognized the number immediately. It was coming from someone at my office. And even though the baby had started to fuss a bit, I didn't want to miss this call. I was due to go back to work in less than a month and figured it was a colleague calling to give me the lowdown on who was fooling around with whom, which editor had gone off the deep end, and what over-the-top celeb demands were throwing the staff into a tizzy. Such is the life at a celebrity news magazine, and I was desperate to get back in the fray.

That excitement, however, evaporated as soon as the phone hit my ear. I heard a teary, nasally voice on the other end. "Ericka," my beloved boss sniffled. "Oh, Ericka. I'm sorry . . ." Too distraught to continue the conversation herself, she passed the receiver to an HR representative who quickly informed me I was being "laid off." Ever imagine what it would feel like to be suspended in a vat of thick, gooey hand sanitizer? Well, that's how I felt.

Everything was heavy around me. I understood what was happening, but I didn't want to believe it. I thought, *What am I if not a* People *magazine writer?* I had done nothing else for a decade. It was no secret the company was tanking. This was 2008 after all, and the entire publishing industry was like the *Titanic*. It was definitely going down, and when it did, there would be mass casualties. For months, *The New York Times* and other papers foretold of the massive cuts needed to keep the place afloat. Still, I felt safe. I was on maternity leave, and who gets fired on maternity leave? Isn't this illegal? Turns out, it's not. Every year, millions of women are lulled into a womb-induced sense of job security. Yet a growing number are finding that their jobs are not safe at all.

The Equal Employment Opportunity Commission received 3,174 complaints from new moms in 2017.[1] The cases include women, like myself, who had been let go, and situations where they were denied promotion, demoted, forced out, or made to take a pay cut. What about the laws that are supposed to protect new moms, you ask? They are not as powerful as you think. "So many people believe the law says you can't do this, but in real life, it's not that simple," warned attorney Susan Crumiller, who founded a New York City–based feminist litigation law firm. "It's not black-and-white."

How Did We Get Here?

Our legal protections have proven to be flimsy at best, though the law certainly suggests otherwise. The Pregnancy Discrimination Act (PDA) of 1978 was the first federal mandate to explicitly protect pregnant employees. It came during a time when unfair treatment was masked under a veil of concern: "We wouldn't want someone in your condition to strain yourself," or "It's just not safe for you to be here." Under the PDA, companies with fifteen or more employees are required to treat pregnancy like all other short-term disabilities, and women cannot be demoted, overlooked for promotion, or let go because they are expecting or might become pregnant. Despite the law and all its promise, pregnancy discrimination remains widespread. Victims, representing every industry, race, ethnicity, and state, reported being denied even minor accommodations, like more frequent bathroom breaks or being allowed to carry a water bottle with them throughout the day. It certainly doesn't get better after baby arrives.

When the Family Medical Leave Act (FMLA) was enacted in 1993, it was heralded as a historic day for women and families. The FMLA requires employers to hold your job for twelve weeks of unpaid leave. This is the part of the law most of us remember. But there are some conditions that leave many working mothers vulnerable. Your job will be held if, and only if, you have worked there more than a year, you work full time, and the company employs more than fifty people. Everyone else—people who work for small businesses or work part time—are at the mercy of their employers.

Even if you do qualify, the United States doesn't require companies to provide paid maternity leave. Shamefully, we are the only developed country that doesn't. Even most small, impoverished nations provide pay to new parents. To put it in perspective, moms in Haiti, arguably one of the poorest countries in the world, are guaranteed six weeks of paid leave. New parents in Sweden are allowed 480 days of leave at 80 percent pay. In France, they get sixteen weeks off with 100 percent of their salary. Russia grants 140 days at full pay. There are 178 other countries where paid leave is guaranteed for working moms. The only ones with a worse track record than the US are Papua New Guinea, Lesotho, and Suriname.

The Protection Women Really Need

Some private companies have stepped up and made policies providing paid family leave. New parents at Netflix, for example, can take off as much paid time as they want after the birth or adoption of a child. Etsy grants twenty-six weeks of paid leave, as does Adobe. At Facebook, you get seventeen weeks of paid bonding time with baby, and Twitter offers twenty weeks. Sounds impressive, but government statistics reveal just 17 percent of workers in the private sector are getting a paid leave benefit and 88 percent have access to unpaid leave.[2] But being unpaid for two months is the least of our worries when we may not have a job to return to. Most women rely on the FMLA to ensure they will have the same position or one with equal pay and benefits once they return from parental leave. In actuality, other research shows only 56 percent of workers in private sector jobs (meaning nongovernmental employees) are covered.[3] Even if you are, hiring managers can exploit little-known (at least to most expectant moms) loopholes that allow them to give women the axe when on maternity leave. You see, a woman cannot be fired because she is pregnant or on leave, but it is perfectly legal to hand out pink slips for one of these three reasons:

WORKPLACE BEHAVIOR. After years of great performance evaluations, you may return to learn that an office review has unearthed a serious offense that took place before going on maternity leave. This could range from improper use of company time, poor performance on a particular project, an inappropriate interaction with coworkers, and other "legitimate reasons" for writing you up and building a case for ultimately letting you go.

JOB ELIMINATION. This is one of the most common excuses for getting rid of a parent, according to Crumiller. Your position can simply be eliminated as part of a company reorganization. In many cases, they will just change what used to be your title and put someone else in the position.

COMPANY-WIDE LAYOFFS. The horrendous economic conditions in the United States have resulted in millions of layoffs in the last decade. The COVID-19 pandemic certainly made those numbers skyrocket in 2020. Unfortunately, new parents aren't immune.

I was the victim of that later category, being among six hundred employees who found themselves suddenly jobless. I'm sure it didn't help that I had taken an extended leave. My son was born six weeks premature and was in the NICU for the first month of his life. What followed was a myriad of health concerns typical of a preemie, and I wanted to stay home until I felt he was healthy and strong. I certainly wasn't the first woman at the company to do this. In years past, new mothers had taken off as much as a year, so I thought nothing of adding a couple extra months.

Colleagues urged me to sue, but I had no interest in being tied up in court with a publishing behemoth. Instead, I took the incredibly generous severance package they offered and moved on. Later, I learned my story became a cautionary tale among staff. Some women contemplating extending maternity leave opted not to for fear the powers that be would "Ericka Sóuter me."

Janis, a former media executive, was similarly shaken after the birth of her first child. When she refused to return to work at a media company just four weeks into her maternity leave, she was abruptly fired even though her boss had agreed to a three-month leave. "I was a single mom with a new baby," she said, still blistering at the memory. "It was devastating. The company was being bought, so firing me wasn't illegal, just unethical. Men are applauded for having families, but new moms are demoted, forced out, or fired."

Many times these perfectly legal justifications can mask an unspoken yet insidious bias toward working mothers. A 2003 study published in the *Harvard Women's Law Journal* explored the "maternal wall," which is the notion that once we become mothers, we are considered far less devoted or capable than childless women.[4] If the glass ceiling is the invisible barrier that keeps us from reaching certain levels of professional success, the maternal wall is the rickety, old elevator that stops many floors short of even that. In American work culture, the ideal employee doesn't take parental leave when a child is born, doesn't require special breast pumping rooms, doesn't need flexible work schedules, and they certainly don't need to take a day off for school snow closures. Many moms complained of the icy stares from coworkers and annoyed looks from managers when they had to dash out because their child had thrown up or had a fever and needed to be picked up immediately. In many environments, there is a complete lack of empathy for the women who are attempting this maddening juggling act.

It's a familiar feeling for working moms across multiple fields. There is a fear that you will lose your standing if you take too much time off. *Will my job be there for me? Will I still be considered for promotion? Will I still be respected?* These were common worries among the women I spoke with. One lawyer refused to take a maternity leave because, "If I did, other lawyers would steal my clients, and I know I wouldn't have been taken as seriously," she said. She was back at her desk two weeks after delivering. Her concern about how mothers are viewed in the workplace is not an exaggeration.

About six months after I started a writing job at another magazine, I told a supervisor that I needed to leave early because I wasn't feeling well. Her response: "Oh God. You aren't pregnant again, are you?" Needless to say, I was taken aback because, one, I had never been a pregnant employee there, and two, I am pretty sure that was illegal for her to say. These passive-aggressive digs make for a very tense and often hostile-feeling work environment.

A Harvard Business School grad lamented that peers at her male-dominated marketing company clearly thought her IQ took a nosedive after she gave birth. Her expertise was respected until she added mother to the résumé. She could feel the difference as soon as she returned from maternity leave. Though she had been an effective leader for years, she no longer felt valued or, frankly, wanted there. Meghan, an insurance industry executive, found her ability to do the job continually questioned by her boss. "He would ask, 'Can you really handle this job with *two* kids?'" she recalled. It seemed to make no difference that she was a top performer and continued to win industry awards. Meghan, like so many women, languished under the assumption that there is no way a woman with children can maintain the same work habits or put in the same amount of time. It's the reason some women are reluctant to even bring up their children at the office. The fear is that we will be judged or penalized because of this other set of responsibilities. It even has a name on social media: #secretparenting. These are the moms who try to stealthily sneak out at 5:00 to make it to daycare pickup or the soccer game.

Is it any wonder women fear that their new-mom status makes them more expendable? Before children, you may have been willing to sign back on to work emails as soon as you got home, work late, or travel last minute if needed. But there is an unspoken understanding that this will change once you return, and there are probably plenty of child-free employees who can fill your shoes. It's not fair, but it's the reality of our situation.

The Cost of Leaning Out

It's the kind of dismal realization that terrifies any working mother looking for a new job. It's especially daunting for those trying to reenter the workforce after years at home. According to a survey of parents conducted by professional networking site LinkedIn, about half of mothers pause their careers after having children.[5] A former assistant district attorney recently found herself in that uncomfortable position. She happily "leaned out" to raise her son. Now that he's seven and completely unappreciative of her hovering, she is itching to get back to work. "I've done the mom thing long enough," she quipped. "I need a job." Her résumé has been updated; she's applying to positions on job sites, making connections via LinkedIn, and more importantly, networking. Until recently, her biggest concern was that she had been professionally dormant for too long, but the perception of working moms is an even higher hurdle.

I tagged along for a casual coffee meeting that this mother had with an executive friend who worked for a large company and happened to have children at the same school. At best, she hoped for helpful tips and maybe a few numbers to call. What she got was a reality check. The conversation started off lively enough with school gossip (the latest class bullies, the meanest teachers, and that outrageous tuition hike), and then talk shifted to the climate that a mother seeking work will undoubtedly face. The exec was candid about the major issue with hiring moms. "You know you are going to be dealing with mind share," she casually offered.

"Mind share?" I interjected quizzically, never having heard the phrase before.

"Work is going to be fighting for your attention," she explained. "You don't worry about that with men." When I asked if she thought "mind share" was a barrier in her own career, she confessed, "I'm lucky enough to have a husband who works from home and takes care of all that school stuff." If only we all were so lucky.

The LinkedIn study also found that more than one-third of mothers who are back after a career break say they struggled to get hired. Stella, a mother of two, feared that kind of bias as she interviewed for jobs in the finance industry. As her family's breadwinner, it was critical she find work after being laid off. Knowing the bias she would face, she lied about her children's ages, making them slightly older. The presumption, she hoped, would be that school-age children would be less needy than toddlers. She also hid the fact that she was in the middle of a divorce. "If they knew I was divorcing, I'm not sure they would have even considered me," she added. "A red flag would go up—SINGLE MOM!"

One human resources executive shared the story of a new hire that didn't mention she was a mother until after she signed her employment contract. "I had no less than five long meetings with this woman, and she went on and on about her husband and not one word about children," she said with a laugh. "I was speaking with her a few weeks after she started, and she said something about her kids. She noticed the surprised look on my face and apologized for keeping it a secret. 'Now that I know you, I see having a family wouldn't have mattered,' she said."

Fears of being displaced or rejected wouldn't be an issue if we lived in a society that revered mothers as much as it pretends to. A 2008 study published in the *Journal of Applied Psychology* found that hiring managers eliminated female applicants with children more often than those without.[6] Parental status, however, did not affect decisions about male applicants. In fact, research shows that when men become fathers, they typically get raises (on average, about a 6 percent increase).[7] Not so for women. While the overall gender pay gap is decreasing nationwide, the pay gap related to motherhood is increasing, according to research by University of Massachusetts–Amherst professor Michelle Budig, who has studied the pay gap for fifteen years.[8] Unmarried, childless women earn 96 cents for every dollar a man earns while married mothers earn 76 cents. It's costing us $16,000 a year in lost wages, according to census data analyzed by the nonprofit advocacy organization National Women's Law Center.[9]

A Stanford University study found that fathers are the most desirable employees, followed by child-free women, child-free men, and lastly, mothers.[10] In general, fathers were considered more stable and committed despite the fact that working moms have proven to be the most productive members of the workforce.

Just as surprising is the fact that female hiring managers demonstrated as much bias against working mothers as men did. Most of us assume other women will understand the plight or be empathetic. Many were appalled to read company president Katharine Zaleski's confession about how she and other execs once treated working moms:

> As a manager at the *Huffington Post* and then the *Washington Post* in my midtwenties, I committed a long list of infractions against mothers or said nothing while I saw others do the same. I secretly rolled my eyes at a mother who couldn't make it to last-minute drinks with me and my team. I questioned her "commitment" even though she arrived two hours earlier to work than me and my hungover colleagues the next day. I didn't disagree when another female editor said we should hurry up and fire another woman before she "got pregnant." I scheduled last-minute meetings at 4:30 p.m. all of the time. It didn't dawn on me that parents might need to pick up their kids at daycare . . . For mothers in the workplace, it's death by a thousand cuts—and sometimes it's other women holding the knives.[11]

I appreciated Zaleski's public mea culpa. It was brave. She saw the error of her ways once she had children and found herself in the same position as those poor moms she tortured all those years earlier. Sadly, that kind of vitriol is still widespread.

As a result, Crumiller is seeing more and more women seeking help before they even reveal their pregnancies to employers. "The biggest concern is job security," she explained.

"They may be up for promotion and don't want their boss to know they are pregnant because they won't get it. Or they are worried that once they tell the boss, their job duties will change and they are going to be effectively demoted." There are also a number of cases where a client has worked out plans for a leave, but their boss has either said or hinted that their position may not be there when they return. Those are scenarios the legal experts at A Better Balance, a work and family legal center that has offices in New York and Nashville, has also seen with alarming frequency.

A 2016 report by the Center for WorkLife Law at the University of California, Hastings College of the Law has found a 269 percent increase in caregiver discrimination lawsuits in the last decade.[12] And experts suggest that those official complaints don't reflect the true breadth of the situation. Many women won't come forward out of fear of retribution from a current or former employer. One bad reference can ruin a career, and the troublemaker brand is almost impossible to shake. A dad who works in finance shared that he was considering hiring a very talented woman until he got wind she had filed a discrimination suit against a former employer. He immediately dropped her from consideration.

It's clearly a systemic problem. Bright Horizons, which runs one thousand daycare centers and preschools nationwide, released a study that revealed that 41 percent of employed Americans believe that working moms are less devoted to their work. More than one-third of respondents judged mothers negatively for needing flexible schedules.[13] Is it any surprise that the number of women who feared telling their boss they were pregnant doubled from 12 percent in 2014 to 21 percent in 2019?[14]

I'm not going to pretend that women's priorities don't change. They do. It's not all about career anymore, and we are given the monumental task of figuring out a way to achieve in two equally demanding but completely disparate strata—work and family. Here's the thing: we do figure it out. Motherhood is actually the best training ground for dealing with difficult personalities and high-pressure situations. Just ask anyone with a toddler. Being a mother has given me the patience of Job. Seriously. It's easy to see why moms make exceptional employees and leaders: we are often good listeners, calmer in a crisis, more diplomatic, and better team players. Studies have shown that parents in general are more productive workers.[15] Still, the bias persists and so does our fear of calling it out.

There is certainly a risk but also potential for great reward and validation for those brave enough to file charges. In recent years, juries were more inclined to award large settlements if gender bias was involved. According to data from the Center for WorkLife Law, plaintiffs who sue in federal court charging family responsibilities discrimination won two-thirds of the cases that actually went to trial.[16] Clearly, something very bad is happening to women in the workplace, and the courts are trying to rectify it. All this begs the question, how can you protect your job after you become pregnant? It's possible if you play it smart. Follow these steps before, during, and after maternity leave to escape the Motherhood Penalty.

YOUR NEW TO-DO LIST

Leading Up to Maternity Leave

MAKE IT CLEAR THAT YOU UNDERSTAND THE LAW. If possible, engage the topic in a positive tone. Crumiller suggests saying something along the lines of: "I am so happy I work for a place where everyone respects the laws and my rights. I am so excited because I know we are going to be able to work something out where I am protected and you get to keep me. And I look forward to continuing to do excellent work for you for a long time."

KNOW YOUR VALUE. Spend time figuring out all the ways that you contribute to the office. Consider asking work friends to weigh in because they may remember things you haven't noted. Make sure your superiors know the positive way you influence day-to-day operations.

UPDATE YOUR RÉSUMÉ. If you have been at the same company for a while, you likely haven't taken a look at your résumé in years. Now is the time to insert the most up-to-date details while they are fresh in your mind.

SEND CONTACTS AND WORK EVALUATIONS TO YOUR HOME COMPUTER. If you are let go while still out of the office on leave, you won't have access to these all-important documents. You will need those contacts for your next career move, and those evaluations may come in handy if you have to take legal action.

During Your Maternity Leave

DON'T GO COMPLETELY MIA. Stay abreast of the latest company news, keep in contact with your boss via the occasional email, and chat with colleagues once in a while. Even sporadic communication can give hints to a change in the mood or culture of the office.

BE CAREER SAVVY. If you have the bandwidth, try to engage in work-related activities, like taking online courses. Networking is also a good idea, even if it's simply meeting a colleague or client for a quick coffee. It's great if you can make time for outings, but many new moms are just too exhausted to even muster up the energy for that. If so, read up on your industry and use sites like LinkedIn to grow professional connections. This will be invaluable if you are on the market for a job sooner than you expected.

If You Suspect You Are Being Pushed Out

REACH OUT TO A LAWYER IMMEDIATELY. Most of us don't have an intricate understanding of employment law and how to use it to our advantage. If you are concerned about legal fees, most of these cases are done on a contingency basis (you don't pay if you don't win), or an hourly fee is charged. It may seem like an aggressive move, but rest assured, your employer already has attorneys hard at work on their side. Your lawyer's first step will likely be sending a letter on your behalf. This lets them know you won't passively accept any discriminatory behavior on their part. They will be compelled to forward it on to their attorney who can hopefully talk some sense into them. Having representation can also help in severance negotiations or if you decide to file a formal complaint with the Equal Employment Opportunity Commission. If you don't want to go that route, it's still important to voice your concerns if you are feeling unfair treatment, advises Crumiller. "If they were considering firing you, but they were on the fence and you say, 'I feel like I am being discriminated against because of my pregnancy,' they are less likely to do it and more likely to be scared."

DISCREETLY SPEAK TO COWORKERS. Find out how colleagues were treated during pregnancy and maternity leave and how they dealt with it. Chances are if you are the victim of discrimination, most people in your office are appalled by the situation. They may share critical information that can help your case.

KEEP COPIOUS RECORDS. Write descriptions of specific incidents and conversations with your superiors. Include time, place, date, every person involved, and what was said. You can keep a list or do something as informal as sending a text to a coworker commenting on the way the boss treated you the day before. If they respond, it is now a piece of evidence.

I know the thought of taking legal action is frightening. Experts tell me that the biggest concern women have is fear of being blacklisted. It's important to remember that you are not a troublemaker. This is about your family's financial security. Besides, most employment discrimination cases settle, and as a part of that, it's standard for the company to agree to (1) keep the issue confidential, (2) instruct their employees not to disparage the person, and (3) give a neutral reference.

Just remember, no one should have to worry about job security during one of the most vulnerable times in her life. And know this: you aren't just fighting for a paycheck. According to Save the Children, in countries with longer parental leave periods, children are breastfed for longer, and they are found to have a longer life expectancy.[17] Not to mention the benefits of bonding with your child and having time for your own body to heal. Those are rights worth fighting for.

Three

It Takes a Village
. . . for You

WHAT TO REALLY EXPECT:
You must redefine what friendship
means at this stage of your life.

Do you remember the anxiety you felt walking into the cafeteria alone the first day of junior high, trying to figure out who to sit with? Well, sorry to break this to you, but finding mom friends as an adult can bring those same grade-school insecurities percolating back to the surface. Essentially, you have to approach a bunch of strangers whom you have nothing in common with except for the fact that your uterus was occupied at the same time. That can evoke dread in even the most confident of women. But don't even think about skipping this step.

Moving to a Los Angeles neighborhood full of what she called "breeders," stand-up comedian and new mom Anna was nervous but thought surely she would make some friends. She took trips to the park and even tried a Mommy & Me group but never felt comfortable. "I just didn't fit in," she said. "They were carrying Chloé diaper bags. I can't even afford Chloé for a regular bag, much less my extra one." One mom likened the process of making friends to having a baby without an epidural. Another lamented, "Do I really have to do this? Do I really need mom friends?"

Yes. You will need the support more than ever. That, however, is the wrong question. You need to ask yourself, *What kind of friends do I need? What kind of friend do I want to be in return?* Surrounding yourself with the wrong people can make you as miserable as not having any friends at all. Most moms need the companionship of other women who are going through the same thing. I, for one, needed empathy, not just the sympathetic smile my partner gave me when he got home to find me looking haggard and depleted.

No matter how you fill your waking hours—at the playground or at an office—the fact of the matter is that you are different now, and so is the type of support that you need from the people around you. Expanding your social circle and relying on other women is actually a natural part of your transition into motherhood.

When Your Pre-Kid Posse Doesn't Cut It

Nancy was excited to introduce her friends to her new baby. A no-nonsense New York transplant from Boston, she hung with a solid posse of cool, worldly, Ivy-League educated types. Needy? Never. Desperate? Not in her vocabulary. That is, until motherhood entered her well-sculpted universe. The first of her group to have kids, the others just didn't get it. One of her friends showed up with his three dogs, one of which peed on her floor. He was also hungry and complained there was nothing in her fridge. "I was like, 'I think you need to go,'" she said, rolling her eyes at the memory. She didn't have a single friend who came by offering to help with the baby, do the dishes, or even ask how she was doing. "They loved me but didn't know what my needs were," she said with an uncharacteristic air of sadness. "I just needed them to sit with me for a while. Though to be fair, I wouldn't have gotten it either before I had a kid."

So, here's the thing about new motherhood that very few of us expect: at a time when you are filled with so much hope, love, and joy, you may also experience an overwhelming sense of loneliness and isolation. You will need the kind of support that only another parent can provide.

How Did We Get Here?

When recalling those early days, most women I spoke with lamented the irony of never actually being alone (because of the baby) but feeling so lonesome. One reason many mothers today feel they are "alone in this" has to do with a cultural shift in the way we live out our adult lives. Once upon a time, generation after generation was raised in the same town, oftentimes on the same block. I grew up in a small midwestern city and had many of the same high school teachers my aunts and uncles did. Family was just a phone call or a short drive away, there to step in if my parents needed help. I didn't appreciate how sanity saving that must have been until

I was parenting hundreds of miles away from them all with only paid babysitters at my disposal. Communities of family members and lifelong friends were essentially a safety net of shared values and goals.

My husband often talks about growing up across the street from his grandmother and two houses down from his cousins. If he misbehaved when his parents were not around, another family member would step in and levy a fitting punishment. It was expected. It was appreciated. Another benefit of that geographical closeness is that new mothers were hardly ever alone, being guided and supported by relatives with more experience.

Sadly for most of us, that setup is as out-of-date as a flip phone. It's more likely you were lured away long ago by education or work opportunities and settled in a city far from your hometown. This creates what I have come to call a familial desert. Much like the food deserts in urban areas that don't have a grocery or fresh food market nearby, we have familial deserts all over the country where parents are functioning without the emotional nourishment of extended family. It makes for a very isolating experience. Many of us must create the village that once happened organically.

What is happening to moms is actually endemic of a larger problem—the epidemic of feelings of isolation and disconnection the world over. If you doubt that, consider this: the British government has appointed a Minister for Loneliness to deal with the nine million citizens—including seniors, the career driven, college students, and not surprisingly, new parents—who often or always feel lonely. Similarly, the US insurance company Cigna conducted a research study that revealed that nearly half of Americans report sometimes or always feeling alone or left out. One in four rarely or never feel as though there are people who really understand them.[1]

Worse yet, 40 percent of Americans sometimes or always feel that their relationships are not meaningful and that they are isolated from others. One in five confessed having no one they can talk to.[2] The effects aren't just emotional. Studies have shown that loneliness has a damning effect on the body as well. It's associated with an increased risk of heart disease and obesity and has the same impact on mortality as smoking fifteen cigarettes a day.[3] Most parenting books, magazines, and blogs offer a deceptively simple solution: just go out and find moms, any moms. I have to caution that this is not about finding people. This is about finding the right people.

So You Have a Uterus Too!

The simple fact that two women are both mothers is not a recipe for real kinship. Nancy found it hard to make a sincere connection with the women she met at a moms' group at a local play center despite the shared goal of walking away with a friend, someone to diminish the disorientation and loss of self that consumed her. "Honestly, we were hardly our best selves," she pointed out. "You are kind of your worst self because you are so sleep deprived, weary, in a constant state of worry." She found it nearly impossible to have a real conversation as they all tended to their babies.

Even worse, most moms seem afraid to say anything remotely negative or honest about what they are going through. "Everyone seemed very earnest," she said with a frown. "I think there was this pressure that now I'm a mother, I can't even joke that my kid's an asshole because he kept me up all night. I wouldn't want someone to judge me for saying something like that. I was looking for a little bit of humor and fun. I wanted someone to not be horrified if I said something not so great." She didn't find it. She left without a single number or email and never returned.

Sure, she could have faked it. I heard from many moms who "hated" their moms' groups but felt like it was them or nothing. That is quite simply giving up on the possibility of really profound connections, and they are out there. It just takes a little work to unearth them.

That's not to say you should ignore your bullshit detector. There are times that you know right away you won't vibe with another person. Feeling the pangs of loneliness, Natalie was eager to make friends when her daughter was a couple months old. She found a local group online and was excited for the lunch meet-up they had planned. Arriving at noon, she learned the first rule of mommy group: they don't start on time. Eventually, eight to ten moms trickled in. That's when she learned the second rule of mommy group: apparently you don't actually bring your baby. The other women had left their children with sitters.

"It was a complete disaster," she bemoaned. "It took forever for our food to get there; my baby is freaking out. Once the food does come, I am trying to spoon yogurt and granola in my mouth, and I am spilling it on her head. Then she had a blowout, and it was the first time I changed her in a public restroom. It was everywhere. The worst part, if I had been with women I had naturally bonded with quickly, I would have shared it, laughed over it. It would be like initiation by fire, and we would have bonded from that moment." Sadly, that was not the case. Instead, the women griped about their nannies and night nurses, astonished that Natalie had neither.

As far as she was concerned, she would rather have been out with their nannies. At least they could give her some advice, she thought. She longed to talk to women who would help her feel like what she was going through was normal. Natalie was done with the entire crew when they started talking about not letting the nannies use the "good" Prada and Fendi diaper bags. Instead they saddled the help with cheap ones. "I was like, 'Check please!'" she laughed. "You will let them have your firstborn child but not the nice diaper bag?" While this might have been exactly the right group of women for some, needless to say, these were not Natalie's people. You will undoubtedly meet women who are clearly too snarky or too high energy, too jokey, or too whatever-your-peeve.

Don't Judge a Mom by Her Stained Shirt

In general, however, it's important not to make a snap judgment based on a lousy first impression. Every mom deserves the benefit of a second chance. It takes more than a thirty-minute chance meeting in the park to learn about someone. Sleep deprived, worried, anxious—none of those characteristics scream "fun gal." Beneath that weary exterior could be a person you will come to cherish. The person who also thinks their kid is a little terror.

When I was on maternity leave, I would hang out with the stay-at-home mom who lived down the hall. She was cynical, critical, and endlessly meddlesome. Most of our neighbors couldn't stand her, but I found her interesting and unwittingly comical. At lunchtime, she would always rush back to her apartment because she didn't trust her sitter to heat up nuggets in the oven. She couldn't stand her mother-in-law. ("Why won't she die already?" she complained when the poor woman was in a coma.) And she was absolutely positive our building super hated her (a suspicion confirmed when he refused to accept her holiday tip). Yet, she was the one constant for me other than the baby.

While we were as different as chalk and cheese, I enjoyed our time together. Would we have been friends had I not been at home, going out of my mind with a newborn? No, probably not. I was new to the building, and everyone else I knew was busy with their career-obsessed, non-baby-having lives. How does the saying go? "If you can't be with the one you love, love the one you're with." But what started as companions out of convenience grew into a lovely camaraderie.

I was never more appreciative of her than the day I lost my job. I sat alone with my baby, my shock, and a measure of grief settling in when she called. "Whatcha doing?" she chirped. I told her I didn't feel well, that I couldn't talk, and abruptly hung up. Ten minutes later, there was a knock on my door. There she stood with two lattes in hand.

She whooshed in, told me to sit down, handed me the drink, and then did one of the kindest things anyone has ever done for me. She didn't ask any questions, she just simply went to work. She put Lex down for a nap, tidied up the toys strewn around the living room, washed and sterilized my bottles, and then sat with me. It was a support I didn't realize I needed until it was there.

Quantity Isn't Quality

During a visit with a New Jersey mom group, I wasn't the least bit surprised to hear a mom wonder aloud, "How can I know so many people but still feel so damn lonely?" I could tell by the faces of the other women in the room that the comment resonated with them as well. Our inclination may be to go out and meet more people, but that is far from the cure, according to Shasta Nelson, an expert on friendship and healthy relationships. "Modern-day loneliness isn't because we need to interact more," she explained to me. "It's because we need more intimacy. That lonesomeness is your body saying, 'I want more connection.'" Think quality time with a few friends rather than a bunch of meaningless group outings. This is what Nelson defines as "frientimacy" in her book *Frientimacy: How to Deepen Friendships for Lifelong Health and Happiness.*

If someone were to ask you on a scale of 1 to 10 how fulfilled you were with your friendships, what would you say? Nelson posed that question to six thousand people, and nearly 70 percent of them said they were deeply dissatisfied with their friendships. What she found was an intimacy gap, a stark divide between what we are currently experiencing in our friendships and what we wish we were experiencing. The answer to the problem is to learn how to develop better connections. I love Nelson's very clear formula for lasting friendship: positivity, consistency, and vulnerability.

So let's break it down. Our relationships should be filled with joy, kindness, empathy, affirmation, and of course, laughter. **We need positivity in order to feel truly accepted.** I am so grateful that my friends get my cynicism and self-deprecating sense of humor. We drop off our kids at school, then meet up for coffee and riff on everything from politics to movies to the *Real Housewives*. And it's not about having the same opinion, but rather wanting to hear each other's thoughts. That doesn't mean you can't complain to one another, cry on a friend's shoulder, or even disagree, but for every negative interaction, there should be five positive ones, according to Nelson. Bottom line, there should be more uplifting moments than destructive ones. Your time with friends should leave you feeling good.

The next requirement is consistency. You can meet a person who is a joy to be around, but if you never interact with them in person, on the phone, over text, or even Skype, that's not much of a relationship. This is another argument for not giving up on a potential mom friend too quickly. During Nancy's attempt to make friends, she would assess moms with the technical temerity of the Terminator. If someone appeared too nervous, the words *TOO FRANTIC* flashed before her eyes in big red letters.

Or there was the one who was *MORE OF A HOT MESS THAN ME.* Another woman was *TOO PERFECT.* In truth, those assessments had more to do with her insecurities than any real fault of those moms. We have to be willing to give people a chance.

Countless women I interviewed shared how they grew close to moms they would have never even talked to had they not volunteered for a school fair together, shared a community service project, or if their children didn't happen to be on the same Little League team. These hours logged is how the history is built. This is how you get to know the other person, understand their behavior, and build trust. But the last piece may be the most significant. **Vulnerability is when we share details about our lives.**

We have to be willing to open up about our fears, insecurities, or shame. We also need to reveal the successes, joys, and dreams. Tell stories about our lives, how we grew up, anything that helps others know the real us. "It includes being able to articulate what you are feeling and ask for what you want from somebody else," Nelson described to me. "That is tremendous vulnerability. At the end of the day, we want to feel loved. And we only feel loved if we feel known, and we only feel known if we actually share ourselves."

A Spiritual Connection

There is another type of bond that we often don't think about as new moms. I didn't grow up particularly religious. When people used to ask my mother where our family worshipped, she'd joke, "Saint Mattress." Raised going to church every Sunday of her childhood, she says she encountered far too many hypocrites. She always believed in the power of prayer, but college and grad school taught her to question things, and she longed for a far more accepting God than the one she was taught about. And my father, well, he was a man of science, so God was more of a theory to him than anything remotely tangible. When I went away to college, a Jesuit university with priests as dorm monitors and professors, I started to explore religion and my own relationship with God.

Then I married into a deeply religious family, so there was no question that we were going to raise our kids to be Christians. When our church offered a moms' Bible study group, I eagerly signed up. I was pretty quiet at first, mostly listening to what everyone else said. I couldn't quote scripture or refer to passages like some of the others. I wasn't there yet.

Over time, the group thinned out, and the five of us who remained became a tight-knit little God Squad. Well, that label may be stretching it a bit. I still can't quote many Bible passages with ease. But these women have been my anchors in the darkest, most unsteady moments.

What is so astonishing is how different we are. There is Joann, the older, stalwart matriarch whose faith and life experience give her a sense of compassion unlike any I have ever experienced. Next is Gabriela, whose soft Ecuadorian accent is only matched by the most caring eyes you've ever seen. Her questions always encourage us to share more and explore what we are struggling with. Then there's Allison, whose blue hair suggests a rebel spirit and a bit of a devil-may-care attitude. She is unique and embraces it, a quality that always puts me at ease and makes me feel that no matter how awkward my admission, I am never alone. Finally Sung, who undoubtedly is the sweetest of the group. But that seemingly passive demeanor masks one fierce mama and friend.

We talk about everything from kids and marriage to politics and racism. We support each other through the deaths of loved ones, illness, problem children, and every uphill battle that comes our way. We try to find comfort in each other and in our faith.

When I think about how easy it would have been not to connect with these one-time strangers, I think about the words of a priest. Yes, a priest. "The unity of life among us is even deeper and stronger than the diversity between us," wrote Henri Nouwen in his book *Discernment: Reading the Signs of Daily Life.*[4] In a lot of ways, this should be the golden rule of developing adult friendships, especially among mothers. There is a universality to the experience that we cannot deny. When you cut through appearances and insecurities, what you find are women who are desperate, not only to do a good job taking care of their kids, but for sincere connection and to be loved for who they are.

Anna eventually found her crew eighteen months into motherhood. She was at the park with her two kids when she noticed another mom who had a blanket and asked if she could rest her five-month-old on a part of it. "We started talking and had a great time," Anna recalled. "After that, I met other moms in the neighborhood whom

I was compatible with. No one cared if someone is breast-feeding or using formula. They have really been lifesavers.

"I didn't realize how starved I was for moms with kids the same age and who were dealing with the same stuff. We laugh about things on our text chains, share parenting tips, talk about our sex lives. It became a village in a sense. If someone's partner is out of town and a kid gets sick, one of us will make a run for you. We do things with our kids, and we talk about real things and nobody is embarrassed." And that is essential.

These friendships are very much a two-way street. We want our friends to see who we are (at our best, worst, most worried, most joyful), and we need to see that in them as well. That comes from spending time, opening up, and giving each other support. Without those kinds of relationships, motherhood can be as desolate as a deserted island.

Punching the Clock

All of this takes time, of course. I know, I know. The mere thought of spreading yourself thinner is maddening, but look at it as an investment in your mental health. To make the kind of connections you so desperately want, you have to put in some serious time.

University of Kansas professor Jeffrey Hall discovered how many hours we need to spend with someone in order to forge a real bond. Hall used surveys of college freshmen to learn how their friendships progressed and the time investment required. It takes about fifty hours of quality time together to morph from acquaintance status to that of casual friend. To make the leap to good friend requires ninety hours and (assuming you can still tolerate each other), you will need to log in more than two hundred hours of quality time to actually become close friends.[5] That means it takes the equivalent of working a full-time job for over a month to make a really good friend. *Who has time for that?* you are likely asking yourself. It's not as impossible as it sounds if you consider how easy it can be to while away the hours with someone.

Think about it this way: You probably have made a close pal at work at some point in your life. If you hadn't been forced together ten hours a day, you might never have chosen this person as a friend, but the fact you spend so much time together creates a bond (as long as they are not a total jerk, of course). For moms, this bonding time can be as simple as meeting for coffee, outings to the park, or simple strolls around the block.

Remember, this isn't only about the minutes ticking away on the clock. You are supposed to use these moments to get to know one another on a deeper level, going beneath the surface to find out what she's really about. It's a critical step that if skipped can have you end up feeling alone no matter how many people you are surrounded by.

Your Net Objective

It's important to acknowledge that making new friends can be a challenge at any age. You may never meet *your* kindred spirit or mom crew at the baby boogie music class or the sandbox. Or perhaps you are just too overwhelmed to actually make it out of the house for a playgroup. If so, you will find solace in the fact that those aren't the only ways to find meaningful connection. Many women shared stories of finding like-minded friends on the internet.

Admittedly, our relationship with social media is complicated to say the least. Seeing a friend post a photo of her perfect family on that perfect vacation in that perfect outfit while you feel that your life is spiraling out of control has a damning effect on self-esteem. Even though we are now well aware that what people post is far from reality, it still compels us to make comparisons between our lives and that heavily filtered and posed version of reality. However, social media can be a source of guidance and support for new moms.

Whatever your particular concern may be, I promise there is an online group for you. These virtual friends are an invaluable resource. It's a way for us to find camaraderie, advice, and real connection even when we can't meet in person. I initially joined a few online communities and private Facebook groups to get a sense of what kind of support they offer a mom.

There are a lot of questions about what baby name to choose, the best stroller, sleep training, where to travel with toddlers, and the like. But there are even deeper conversations brewing. They share fears over the pressure to be perfect, concerns about kids with serious medical conditions, suspicions about cheating spouses, nightmare mothers-in-law, and pleas for encouragement when you feel at your wit's end.

When doctors informed April that her then eighteen-month-old son was autistic and would never be able to communicate with her, she was devastated. Feeling help-less and hopeless, she sat in her Andover, Massachusetts, home crying, wondering how the hell she was going to raise her child. Searching the internet, she stumbled across a blog by Carrie Cariello, a mom who writes about raising five kids, one with autism spectrum disorder.

"She saved my life," April shared. "I felt so lost before I read her blog. She talked about the disconnect with her husband, how the other kids feel neglected, seeing her kid go on the short bus for the first time. It was finally a mom's experience I could relate to."

I felt a special kinship with the mom who posted after giving birth to a twenty-five-weeker struggling to survive. I was in her shoes once upon a time. I laughed when another mom asked for advice about teen boys and hygiene. I know that battle is coming. These are intended to be safe, judgment-free spaces. You can swear, admit to despising family members, talk about struggles with mental health. It's a no-holds-barred place to bare your soul. Shaming someone can get you booted. When you feel at your most vulnerable, you can find a group of hundreds, if not thousands, available twenty-four hours a day who can relate.

Pandemic Parenting

These types of communities were especially significant during the coronavirus pandemic. The social distancing mandated by officials was devastating for everyone, but more so for expectant and new moms. Motherhood is already an isolating and anxiety-inducing experience. Muddling your way through those first weeks and months felt like a nightmare with no visits from friends or family, no in-person check-in from a loving doula, no baby showers or Mommy & Me classes or stroller walks through the park.

"I already feel so alone. This makes it worse."

"I just want to be in a room with a friend.
Have a face-to-face conversation."

"What if my baby gets sick?"

"When will this end?"

Facing an unusual situation like this, it's more important than ever to vent and share struggles. You have to find an outlet, a place to get a pat on the back and hear, "You got this, mom. You will get through this." The first step in identifying the right virtual support group for you is to do a web search. Among the most popular websites are Meetup, CircleMoms, CafeMom, Mamapedia and BabyCenter. One thing I've learned from my own experience is that friends feed an emotional need that is different from what we get from a spouse or our children.

A small group of my closest mom friends set up a standing video call every night at 5:00. Each day we helped each other navigate this new normal. From the mundane—What's everyone making for dinner?—to the consequential—How will we keep our spirits up and marriages intact? It's a life lesson we never imagined enduring, but we're glad we have each other to turn to.

Whether it's a global crisis or a move away from everything and everyone that is familiar, we need to maintain those connections, especially if we are worried, frightened, and unsure. Ultimately, experiences like this strengthen you in ways you never imagined. It's critical to remember that we are all alone together.

Beware of the Toxic Mom Friend

Just as we have to learn to cultivate friendships, we have to know when to let them go. When people think of toxic moms, they envision a grown-up version of the high school mean girl who sets the standard for cool and ices out anyone she deems unworthy. It's not always so obvious in real life. Often we ignore the signs because we are so needy for a connection, a crew. Though, over time, you may find that this friendship you so desperately wanted causes more harm than good. It's not easy to cut off any relationship, but ask yourself the following:

Are you starting to feel excluded on purpose?

Does she say hurtful things?

Is she overly critical of you?

Is she sharing things you told her in confidence?

Does she say nasty things about other
friends when they are not around?

It's important to take stock of how you feel after you are with that friend. Negative relationships and constant drama will drain you of energy and make you feel judged. I was discussing these scenarios with Naphtali Roberts, a Burbank, California-based therapist and mother, and it triggered her own aha moment.

After our first interview, she happened to have a reunion with her old mom group. "I used to spend every single day with these women when I was a stay-at-home mom," she explained during our follow-up conversation. "I had not seen them for a really long time, and there was so much under-the-surface judgment on different life choices and condescending compliments. I think they were why I was so unhappy when I was at home. Because I have had so much distance and gotten so much stronger with who I am, it doesn't impact me the same way. The people you surround yourself with greatly impact your mood and your mental state and your belief in your level of competency even."

According to friendship expert Shasta Nelson, the next steps may not necessarily be to break up with them, but rather break up with your expectations of them. A lot of people lack a basic awareness of what comes out of their mouths. Or it could be you are having one of those sensitive days when you take something the wrong way.

The point is that we don't want to drop a friend too hastily. Give people a chance, Nelson urges. First try identifying which of the three friendship requirements are missing and attempt to repair it. We shouldn't just dismiss the investments we have already made. "A lot of our loneliness is because we keep starting over," suggests Nelson. "If we don't want to work through the hard parts and do the work, all we will be left with are shallow relationships." If something perceptible has shifted, drop them from the top of your "call with good news list" or stop sharing your most intimate secrets. Not everyone has to be a BFF. There is a huge gulf between removing some-one from your life and being their bestie.

Sadly, there are some former friendships that are beyond repair. It's painful to let go of a friend, especially one that was once valued. You may find that differences present themselves over time. I still think about the loss of a particular mom friend I spent a lot of time with during those first years of motherhood. We bonded commiser-ating about the struggles of careers, marriages, and kids. Oftentimes after work, we would get the kids in their pj's, meet at one of our apartments, and have a drink while they played. It was sanity saving. As our children got older, differences in values and parenting styles started caus-ing a lot of tension. I was trying to hold on to the way our friendship used to be even though things had clearly changed. Our get-togethers felt strained, and I stopped sharing much about my life in general. It didn't help that both my husband and I took issue with some of her child's behavior. That's a sore spot with any parent and under-standably so. She finally stopped speaking to me after I complained about a prank her child had played that scared our babysitter. This taught me two very important lessons about having adult mom friends: you have to have some shared values, and you should not let your friendship be impacted by whether your children get along.

I'm sure she thought my husband and I were uptight and annoying. I didn't appreciate her laissez-faire attitude toward certain behaviors, and I imagine she and her spouse felt very judged. I am positive that neither of us felt like we were being very good friends to one another. I have no doubt that she is a great friend to other women, but we ultimately were not the right fit. That said, as adults, we should be able to see former friends in group settings and still be cordial. You never want to be bratty or mean. Much like what we tell our children, the goal is always to be kind.

Dumping a Friend the Right Way

Here is where I went wrong in the process: Essentially, I withdrew because I was too cowardly to tell her how I was feeling, which was the worst thing I could have done. "You need to have an honest conversation if you feel like someone is being toxic," explained Maryellen Mullin, a San Francisco–based marriage and family therapist and founder of the website Messy Parenting. She recommends starting the chat as follows:

I'm sure this isn't your intention, but this is how I feel about . . .

You may get a defensive response like, "I am not responsible for your feelings," or an apologetic one like, "I didn't mean to make you feel that way." The point is to allow them to respond and then ultimately follow your gut as to whether you should stay in the friendship. Also give yourself the space to mourn the death of that friendship. I certainly did. That mom once meant a lot to me, but if a relationship causes negativity in your life, it's time to move on. Think about your relationships with each woman in your life. Are you encouraged by her words and actions? Do you feel supported? Do you leave get-togethers feeling uplifted or more depleted than when you arrived? It's a painful realization but one you can't ignore. Your goal is to focus on and build upon those relationships that lift you up, feed your soul and, when it's called for, keep you sane.

YOUR NEW TO-DO LIST

Build Your Mom Tribe

1. **Make the approach.** Most people don't enjoy this part, but it's absolutely necessary. Refusing to do this is like going to the grocery store and expecting the food to magically find its way into your cart. Unless you are Harry Potter, that ain't happening. Suppress that inner introvert and go up to a mom pushing a stroller in your neighborhood, at the park, or baby yoga class. And remember you can also make connections online.

2. **Linger at school drop-off and pickup.** Lots of moms, myself included, find this is the perfect time to chat with other parents and make plans to get together.

3. **Volunteer for school events.** I had never even touched a glue gun until a mom asked me to join her decorating team for the school holiday fair. I adopted some serious crafting skills and developed some of my closest friendships.

4. **Schedule playdates.** Lots of them. This isn't just a time for kids to connect. You and

that other mom can spend an hour sharing bedtime war stories, issues with your spouses, and other common parenting battles.

5. **Don't turn down an invite.** Don't say no to coffee or lunch with a mom just because she doesn't "seem" like your type. You won't get to know anyone unless you give her a chance.

6. **Don't give up.** You may not find your go-to group the first week or month, but they are out there.

Think of these initial meet-ups as informal interviews. Do you have anything in common? Do you like her sense of humor? Does she even have a sense of humor? You won't click with everyone you encounter, but there is bound to be a kindred spirit for you out there.

Grown-Up Rules of Friendships

- Your friends don't all have to be BFFs. We have this tendency to feel that we have to befriend entire groups. It's fine to have confidantes who don't know or even like each other. Our friends can feed different parts of our soul and serve different purposes in our lives.

- It's okay for friends to be critical of one another. It's human. You just have to ask yourself where it comes from. A friend who is concerned about your marriage may sound critical of your spouse, but it could be because she wants you to feel supported. However, a person who is always shooting down your ideas or making put-downs masked in humor is not a friend.

- Time together doesn't always have to be a grand event. Quality time can also be watching the *Real Housewives* (yes, I am obsessed with the show) together or even sitting in silence. Sometime we just need the presence of someone who cares.

- Your kids do not have to be besties. They don't even have to be friends. If your friendship is reliant on this requirement, what happens when your kids grow apart or start to dislike each other? A good foundation has more to do with you than with your children.

- You should feel heard. Good friends listen. You never want to feel as though the person you are sharing with is trying to one-up your story or compare triumphs or defeats.

- Making plans with your friend should bring a smile to your face. If you dread hanging out, that's a clear sign of a problem.

Compatibility Test

Does this person have a similar sense of humor?

Do we share a similar parenting philosophy?

Is she a good listener?

Do we look forward to time together?

Do we have shared values?

Does she flinch when I reveal the parts of myself that don't match those perfectly posed Instagram shots?

Is she comforting?

Do we have a shared experience?

Is she supportive?

Can we disagree with one another without causing a major rift?

Can we offer constructive criticism to each other without anger?

Your friendships have surprise benefits for your kids too.

Having buds isn't just good to you. It also has a positive effect on your kids. A 2019 study that appeared in the *Journal of the American Medical Association* found that moms who have strong friendships have children with better language, motor, socioemotional, and adaptive behavioral skills.[6] The exposure can help socialize your baby early on and teach them what good, supportive relationships look like.

Four

The Real Mommy War

WHAT TO REALLY EXPECT:
Strive for understanding
rather than acceptance.

Motherhood would be great if it wasn't for, you know, other mothers," quipped Jackie, a New York City mother of two. Her words were as funny as they were painfully accurate. Although we had just been discussing the impact of friendships, all is not roses in the way women treat one another. We can't have an honest discussion about motherhood without addressing the whole notion of the mommy wars. While some people like to say it's overblown hype, my conversations with women certainly proved otherwise. Even Jackie's comment came on the heels of a particularly nasty run-in with a mom during school drop-off.

A business owner, event planner, and neighborhood activist, she evokes an image of a Tasmanian devil cartoon, always in motion. So, when her babysitter unexpectedly resigned, it turned her morning into a frenzied mess. In a near sprint, she weaved her way through the crowded city sidewalks, a kid clasped in each hand, thinking about the crazy day of work that lay ahead and wondering how the hell she was going to find a new nanny. Sweat-soaked, she managed to drag her children through the doors before the final bell, but accidentally clipped another mom in the process. "Sorry! My sitter just quit and I'm a bit crazed," she breathlessly offered this stay-at-home mom she had often exchanged pleasantries with.

What she expected was an empathetic smile and maybe even an encouraging, "Hang in there, girl!" The reaction she got, however, left her bruised and embittered. "Finally learning what it's like to be a mom, huh?" the mom smirked.

How Did We Get Here?

That's exactly the kind of us-versus-them mentality that has been the hallmark of the mommy wars since their inception. A 1989 *Texas Monthly* article is often credited with first defining the issue. "Working moms view stay-at-home moms as idle and silly, traitors in the battle to encourage men to assume more responsibility at home. Stay-at-home moms view working moms as selfish and greedy, cheating their own children out of a strong maternal bond," wrote Jan Jarboe Russell in the piece entitled "The Mommy War."[1] Yes, the vitriol goes both ways.

I found it very telling that just a couple weeks later during a follow-up conversation with Jackie, she made a biting remark about a stay-at-home-mom neighbor. This woman had three kids, but was adamant that she would never hire a sitter. It's something she and her husband were not comfortable with. "She likes to say she does everything herself, but her parents are there to help her. That's not doing it all," Jackie offered without a hint of irony.

It was very reminiscent of Leslie Morgan Steiner's 1996 *Mommy Wars: Stay-at-Home and Career Moms Face Off on Their Choices, Their Lives, Their Families*, which shared tales from both sides. Like heavyweight boxers in the ring, each essay was a punishing blow to the other side. As contributor Page Evans describes it, "Sort of a West Side Story, fighting it out behind each other's backs instead of in back alleys. The Sharks and the Jets. Stay-at-home moms vs. working moms. Bored. Guilty. Bored. Guilty. Bored. Guilty. I hear fingers snapping and tongues hissing. 'You must feel guilty,' the stay-at-home moms sneers, pulling out her switchblade, taking another job. 'You must be so bored,' the working mom says spitting in disgust."[2]

Despite the fact that in this day and age, most women have to work and more than 70 percent of moms with children under eighteen are in the workforce, there will always be examples of the bake-sale-organizing PTA set squaring off against the stiletto-and-business-suit-clad contingent.[3] Yet it's important to note that this is no longer the defining feud between moms.

The New Battle Lines

Today, the war has expanded to include everything from mothering philosophies to what you feed your child. I would go as far as to say that it's actually not much of a war anymore. It's more like a long list of annoying skirmishes in our race for mothering superiority. We see spanking versus time out, formula versus breast milk, helicopter versus free range, co-sleeping versus crying it out, organic versus anything else. It's endless. Women I interviewed for this book bemoaned feeling judged over not driving the right car, giving solids at five months, carrying a luxury diaper bag or not carrying one. There's even derision over the way we deliver our babies.

A coworker felt sorry for me because I had a C-section. "I would never want to bring a baby into this world pumped with drugs and in a cold hospital," she offered sympathetically. She said it was as though I never *really* experienced childbirth. In turn, I thought there is no amount of money anyone could pay me to endure a homebirth like she did, though I kept it to myself. These statements of opinion become unwitting attacks making us feel insecure or defensive.

Fact is, dealing with other moms can be far more frustrating than those sleepless nights and endless diaper changes could ever be. As many as 61 percent of moms in the United States say they feel judged.[4] This can leave us completely dismayed during an already difficult time of life.

There is no question this pressure is unrelenting. Catherine O'Brien, a marriage and family therapist who facilitates in-person and virtual support groups for mothers in Sacramento, California, told me that it's one of the biggest concerns among the women in her sessions. "There is so much comparison going on out there, as if there is only one right way to parent," she said.

"I have moms who tell me they worry about telling other moms they supplement formula because of judgment that can come with not giving the best to your child. Moms who don't share that they are struggling with postpartum depression or anxiety because they feel like they aren't good enough moms or feel others will think they are weak or just don't love their babies. Moms have told me they weren't allowed to attend playgroups because they didn't live in a certain neighborhood or wear their baby enough."

In an ideal world, we would come up with a way to end this era of combative parenting we have entered. Many have certainly tried. Every few months, I see an admirable campaign calling for moms the world over to stop the mom shaming and end the mommy judgment. Nothing seems to stick.

Like-Minded Moms

Some women have sought solution and solace by limiting their interactions to like-minded social media groups. Moms Who Love Tattoos. Organic Moms. Moms Who Smoke Pot. Free the Nipple Moms. If you have a penchant for something, I promise you can find a community for it. One of the most popular iterations is the uprising of Unicorn Mom groups. These are moms who swear, drink, have a bawdy sense of humor, and don't give a flying you-know-what about what other women think. You can post anything. You can confess anything. Without judgment.

That's a pretty hard restriction to put on human nature. I have to admit, when one member posted that she was up for a porn industry film award and wanted us to weigh in on what she should wear, I formed a few very strong opinions. I couldn't help but wonder if her kids knew. What if other parents in her community found out? Then I wished I were confident enough to even consider doing something like that. This woman was absolutely gorgeous. When it comes to judgment, sometimes we just can't help ourselves.

Winning Is Everything

Part of the problem is that we are so competitive with one another. A woman is never more emotionally vulnerable than when she becomes a mom. Self-esteem issues are certainly at play in Leora Tanenbaum's refreshingly frank *Catfight: Women and Competition*. She even admits that she can't bring herself to spend time with a college friend who lives in the same neighborhood because her apartment is nicer, her kids are better behaved, her career is more glamorous, and her husband is more handsome. "I measure myself against other women," she wrote. "I constantly need to prove my worth, show everyone (especially myself) that I am capable, deserving, a woman who should be paid attention to. At some level, this is an expression of inadequacy. I worry I can never measure up. I am not smart, fashionable, thin, savvy, or maternal enough. The success of another woman translates into my failure. And my success translates into her failure—which makes my success all the more sweet."[5]

Real or imagined, it seems we will find some way to create a sense of competition.

Similarly, in *The Mommy Myth: The Idealization of Motherhood and How It Has Undermined Women,* authors Susan Douglas and Meredith Michaels claim this "intensive mothering is the ultimate female Olympics. We are all in powerful competition with each other, in constant danger of being trumped by the mom down the street or in the magazine we're reading. The competition isn't just over who's the superior mother—it's over who's the best. We compete with each other; we compete with ourselves."[6] It's hard to deny. There is definitely a tendency to one-up each other, even when it's about something negative. I have seen women go toe-to-toe over who has the worst-behaved toddler. It's like, "I will take your painting the walls with permanent marker and raise you a stabbing of a sibling with a pencil."

Are We Wired This Way?

Why are we like this? Plenty of experts blame relational aggression, or RA. At its most basic level, RA is the act of one person or a group emotionally hurting someone or bringing down their social standing. It's words rather than fists that inflict the harsh blows. In *Woman's Inhumanity to Woman,* Phyllis Chesler outlines it as "verbal and indirect aggression among girls and women [and] includes name calling, insulting, teasing, threatening, shutting the other out, becoming friends with another as revenge, ignoring, gossiping, telling bad stories behind a person's back, and trying to get others to dislike that person. Additionally, the formation of exclusive female dyads and cliques begin early in life."[7] It's hard to argue with this. We've been experiencing it since grade school.

I once wrote a blog post for CafeMom with the headline "Are Three-Year-Old Mean Girls Proof Women Are Born Wicked?" Admittedly, that title was clickbait. Of course I don't believe that women are born wicked, but I wanted to spark a real discussion about the way we treat one another. It was inspired by a bullying incident that occurred at my son's preschool. Some girls were bullying another:

"You're not pretty."

"We don't like your hair."

"We don't want to be your friend."

I wondered how children so young already knew how to strike such emotionally charged blows before adolescence, arguably the cruelest period of a girl's life. Yet this behavior can continue into adulthood. The whole thing is even a part of the cultural zeitgeist. How many movies depict warring moms—a schleppy, hot-mess underdog pitted against the perfect, all-powerful, and incredibly bitchy alpha? That can play out in real life, if not nearly as dramatically.

Why aren't we the champions of choice, acknowledging that there are different ways to mother and mother well? First, we need to understand where this judgment comes from. Nothing will make you feel more insecure than motherhood and the endless array of choices you have to make in order to give your child the best care possible. Our greatest fear is that we will do a bad job and mess up our kids in some way. So in many respects, it's natural to take stock of what others do. When we see that a mom has made a different choice than we have, we lash out, feeling as though her choice is some kind of judgment on our own parenting.

I have been guilty of this.

A few years back, I noticed how annoyed I was at mothers who opted for extended breastfeeding. I couldn't stop talking about the mom I met who didn't wean until her son was in the second grade. She told me it was a continued way for them to bond, still I kept thinking, *That kid has a full set of teeth. And sharp ones at that. Why in the world is she breastfeeding him?* I had to ask myself, *Why did I care so much?* It wasn't hard to find the answer with a little bit of self-reflection. Breastfeeding was incredibly difficult for me. I was a bad milk producer, like one of those anemic water fountains, water barely trickling out. I couldn't get either of my boys to latch well. It made me feel like a failure, like I wasn't doing the best for my kids, even though I tried. My subconscious reaction was to lash out against this amazing superfeeder.

Being Judgy Gets a Bad Rap

Judgment is too innate to simply eradicate, but we can change our relationship with the concept. Let's revisit the actual definition of the word. The dictionary defines *judgment* as "the process of forming an opinion or evaluation by discerning and comparing." That doesn't sound so bad, right? Why then have we been conditioned to believe that judging something is such a loathsome trait? Does it have to be an act of cruelty? Only if we let it.

When you form a judgment, you are asserting your own values. You are making a value judgment. You are creating the values by which you and your family live. There is nothing wrong with that. We are all entitled to an opinion. How you deliver that opinion, however, determines your mean girl status. So how do we fix this? We can start by allowing ourselves to disagree with another mom's choice but still respect it. Getting along with one another will require striving for understanding rather than acceptance.

We don't have to adopt that position, opinion, or behavior, but why can't we offer a bit of understanding? I may never be completely comfortable with breastfeeding a child with strong enough teeth to chew steak, but I can support another woman's decision to do it. Her choice has no bearing on my own mothering or experience. That should be the goal. We can be different, but we don't have to be cruel. We don't have to be bullies.

Stop Fearing Judgment

In truth we all spend an inordinate amount of time judging others in every area of our lives. You readily form strong opinions about that coworker who is always late and that friend who always has boyfriend drama. You see a kid shivering in the park and wonder how his mom could forget to bring along a jacket. People are always telling me I need to fatten up my incredibly skinny child. They have no idea how hard I try. The point is it's natural to judge people and situations. This tendency is ubiquitous in our society.

And yes, gossip is a form of judgment, but it doesn't have to have a malicious intent. My friends and I love to dish over morning coffee. Sometimes we are all in agreement; other times it's a debate. There is a form of intimacy that is created by this. The idea is not to be cruel but to relish a form of expression that is natural and even innate. On the other side, we also have to accept that people are not going to agree with us and may form opinions that we don't like about our own choices. That is also perfectly fine—or at least it should be. We have to get over the need for so much approval from people that, quite honestly, don't really matter in the grand scheme of our lives as parents.

For this to really take root in your life, there are certain things you must do. The first is avoid making rash judgments. Despite what we've been taught, first impressions are rarely correct or fair. When my son was in preschool, another mom once mistook me for a nanny. I was pissed. I made all kinds of assumptions about why she thought that, none of which were kind. Does she think every Black woman in the neighborhood is a caretaker? Does she think a Black mom couldn't afford a private preschool? I assigned all kinds of labels to her—insensitive, rude, perhaps even a little prejudiced. In hindsight, I know that my reaction had more to do with my own sensitivities than anything else.

A couple months later, we happened to both be chaperoning a field trip at our kids' school. Forced together, we finally had a chance to talk and bonded rather quickly. We had more in common than I imagined.

To this day, I hate that I was so dismissive of her initially. I could have robbed myself of someone who became a very good friend.

We can relieve a lot of the inner turmoil created by judgment by accepting it's going to happen to us and be done by us. What if we took it a step further and even assigned benefits to the act. If you stop thinking of judgment as one person placing him- or herself above another, it relinquishes a lot of its power. To judge simply means to differentiate. If we didn't have judgment, how would we come up with our own set of beliefs? How would we know what was right for our self and our family?

YOUR NEW TO-DO LIST

- **Accept that judgment is a part of life.** Looking at it any other way gives it entirely too much power.

- **If you feel unfairly judged, don't react.** If someone is being mean-spirited, they are hoping to negatively affect you. And remember, this type of behavior is not about you, but rather the critic's own insecurities.

- **Before you judge someone, ask, "Is this how I would like to be treated?"** Consider the mom's feelings and situation. You should not expect more respect than you are willing to give others.

- **Consider why you feel this way.** Make sure your judgment doesn't come from a bitter or envious place.

- **Don't be vicious.** You never want to derive pleasure from someone else's misfortune and pain.

- **Accept that being a good mom has many definitions.** There is no one perfect way to parent. If that were the case, everyone would be doing it.

- **Avoid mean-spirited moms altogether.** Unless you are mean-spirited too. Then you can be toxic mom twins. Just don't be surprised if no one wants to hang out with you.

- **Remember that you, too, are fallible.** We all have flaws, and we must remember that. Sometimes we find fault in others that we have in ourselves. Don't be a hypocrite.

Five

No Kidding: Why Your Child-Free Friends Think You Are a Jerk

WHAT TO REALLY EXPECT:
Your child-free friends may
feel betrayed by you.

I t doesn't take a genius to know that women's relationships with one another are complicated. When I began interviewing moms, I expected complaints about *other* women. Our temperamental bonds are the cause of the mommy wars. I remember a woman stopped talking to me after I joked that breastfeeding was akin to waterboarding and was happy to pack up my pump after three months. At the time I didn't know she planned to breastfeed her son for at least two years. It's a clear example of needing to know your audience.

Other moms shared stories of being summarily discarded for something as trivial as not using the "right" baby carrier to the more heady decision to go back to work instead of staying home. Yes, we can be a complicated bunch.

We know it, and many of us own it. So I didn't bat an eye over the bottle-versus-breast spats or insecurities born of watching another mom's seemingly perfect life on Instagram.

However, my conversations with women for this book revealed a truly troubling divide among women in general. When the topic of child-free friends came up and how we navigate those relationships, I was surprised to hear a mix of largely negative judgments and emotions. Moms expressed everything from annoyance to pity to rage.

What the F*** Do They Do on Weekends?

Jackie was eager to talk about the frustrations she felt toward a group of longtime, child-free friends. She had known these women for fifteen years, first bonding when they were all single, up-and-coming career women. Understandably, their lives all centered around work, friendship, and fun. That changed when Jackie tied the knot and had kids soon afterward. Now, every time they got together, without fail, she says these women talk about how happy they are not to be tethered by the restrictions of family life. "It's driving me bonkers," Jackie fumed. "These girls—my best friends—they don't get it."

"What exactly do they *not* get?" I asked. I love being a mom, but I can't deny what motherhood must look like to even the casual observer. It most certainly conjures up the image of the frantic, tired, sleep-deprived woman longing for more time for herself. All of us have been *that* woman. Most of us still are. It's not the complete picture, of course, but it's the most visceral image of motherhood in pop culture.

"Yes, there are highs and lows," Jackie continued a bit more defensively than I expected. "But to me, this is what I was meant to be and what I was meant to do. I honestly feel that of all the accomplishments I've had my whole entire life, having kids, by far, is the best thing I ever did. I want them to know that it's awesome and it's fun. It's like all the things you read about in books."

Other reactions to child-free women felt harsher. One mom chided, "What the fuck do these people do with their time? Who do they hang out with on weekends? They have to make friends with twenty-two-year-olds." It was as if a life without children held no value proposition, even by women who lament being overwhelmed, taking hits in their careers, or feeling like they had lost themselves.

What became clear to me is that even in this day and age, most people believe that raising a family is a moral imperative, something everyone should want to do. Those who don't feel this way experience a form of tacit character assassination, even from friends. Descriptions like *narcissistic, clueless, selfish*, and *stupid* were used to describe these women without hesitation. Interestingly, these words weren't meant to be insults but rather expressions of pity. Jackie was betting on the notion that the job success her pals boasted of and the freedoms they so dearly cherished would give way to a more significant dream: marriage and, more importantly, children. If it did not, they would surely regret their choices, living lonely, incomplete lives. It's a perception that dominates our culture, leaving no room for another definition of a fulfilled life, especially for a woman. The harshness of the judgment didn't give anyone pause. They were simply sharing a truth of a common perspective.

The Hate Is Real

A study published in *Sex Roles: A Journal of Research* took a look at modern attitudes toward people who reject parenthood. Indiana University psychology professor Dr. Leslie Ashburn-Nardo gave 204 psychology students short passages about married adults and asked them to rate their feelings toward that person and their perception of that person's level of fulfillment. The only detail that changed was the subjects' gender and whether or not they had chosen to have kids. The child-free were consistently viewed as less fulfilled. Even more telling, there was a sense of moral outrage, anger, and disgust directed at this group.

Why such strong reactions for people they have never actually met? They bucked the cultural norm, wrote Dr. Ashburn-Nardo in her paper. "People who violate social role expectations based on widely shared cultural stereotypes are subject to perceivers' backlash, such as social and economic sanctions and sabotage. This backlash is justified in the minds of perceivers because the targets are thought to have brought it upon themselves by not fulfilling their expected roles."[1]

It seems like such an antiquated mode of thinking in modern society, but here we are. The question is why do we still think this way? Some of you may be wondering why you should care about this issue. Does it really have any bearing on motherhood? Yes. More than you think. These friendships forged long ago have shaped much of our young lives. They can still hold a lot of significance if we continue to nurture them.

How Did We Get Here?

It's our own parents and extended family that teach us the value of parenthood. Even in my own home, I noticed my husband saying to our then eight-year-old, "When you have children of your own . . ." or "When you are a dad . . ." Later, when I asked Caleb, "What if Lex doesn't want kids?" he was clearly dismayed by the suggestion. "Don't say that, of course he will want a family," he shot back in a way that sounded more like a hope than a certainty. The idea of having kids someday is a natural expectation in our culture. It's easy to see the seeds of this belief in religion. More than 70 percent of the US population identifies as Christian. Judaism, the second largest religion in the country, is practiced by 1.9 percent.[2] The first commandment God gave to Adam? "Be fruitful and multiply." Even the religious doctrines of classical Islam, Hinduism, and Confucianism espouse the virtue of marriage and big families. And though many scholars note a decline in the number of devout worshippers, there is still an undeniable impact on our views. Even non-Catholics adore Pope Francis, widely considered the most open-minded pontiff in history. His openness to Muslim migrants, deep concern over the environment, and a less harsh tone on divorce and homosexuality has earned him the label of "heretic" by more conservative believers.

Interestingly, there is one area where he shows no compromise: living child-free. "A society with a greedy generation, that doesn't want to surround itself with children, that considers them above all worrisome, a weight, a risk, is a depressed society. The choice not to have children is selfish. Life rejuvenates and acquires energy when it multiplies: It is enriched, not impoverished," he told a 2015 crowd in St. Peter's Square.[3] There is that "selfish" tag again; this time lobbed on a world stage. As though making a well-thought-out decision to forgo having children because of your personal needs and circumstance is a more selfish act than having a child you are not prepared for. But this is the attitude that your child-free friends face every day.

There is also a sense of social responsibility that guides our belief that everyone should be willing to have a baby. As we explored earlier, rearing children was once seen as the primary, if not only substantive, contribution a woman could offer the world. To sell this, a damaging illusion was created, according to early feminist Leta Hollingworth. In her 1916 paper "Social Devices of Impelling Women to Bear and Raise Children," she explains how those in power worked hard to gaslight the would-be mothers of America:

> The pains, the dangers, and risks of childbearing
> are tabooed as subjects of conversation. The
> drudgery, the monotonous labor, and other
> disagreeable features of child rearing are minimized
> by "the social guardians." On the other hand, the
> joys and compensations of motherhood are

magnified and presented to consciousness on every hand. Thus the tendency is to create an illusion whereby motherhood will appear to consist of compensations only and thus come to be desired by those for whom the illusion is intended.[4]

Even men of science backed up the notion that all women were meant to breed. Hollingworth noted that the "medical profession insistently proclaims desire for numerous children as the criterion of normality for women, scornfully branding those so ill-advised as to deny such desires as 'abnormal.'"[5] Case in point was this article that appeared in a New York newspaper on November 29, 1915:

> Only abnormal women want no babies. Trenchant criticism of modern life was made by Dr. Max G. Schlapp, internationally known as a neurologist.
> Dr. Schlapp addressed his remarks to the congregation of the Park Avenue M. E. Church. He said, "The birth rate is falling off. Rich people are the ones who have no children, and the poor have the greatest number of offspring. Any woman who does not desire offspring is abnormal. We have a large number, particularly among the women, who do not want children. Our social society is becoming intensely unstable."[6]

Later, when the country suffered severe population losses during war, the government encouraged families to procreate. The result was the post–World War

II baby boom and the birth of that perpetually happy homemaker image of the '50s and '60s. The women's movement and the advent of the Pill should have obliterated the status quo, but there were limits to progress. In *The Baby Matrix: Why Freeing Our Minds from Outmoded Thinking about Parenthood & Reproduction Will Create a Better World*, Laura Carroll writes, "While the movement empowered women in a number of ways, it did not challenge childbearing directly. The empowerment that came from access to birth control focused more on their power to choose when to have a child, not whether to have a child at all."[7]

Mothers Need Not Apply

In modern times, it seems this pressure has not relented. Though, to get a real sense of its effect, I needed to spend time with women who did not have children. No better place for that than the inaugural NotMom Summit, a conference that aimed to support and embrace women who were child-free by choice or by chance.

In the days leading up to it, I wasn't sure what to expect. "That's an odd thing to celebrate," my husband remarked when I told him about my upcoming trip. "Why?" I asked, a bit annoyed. He just shrugged. Of course we both knew the answer. Every woman is supposed to want to be a mom, and if she doesn't, she should. Once at the summit, however, I was overwhelmed by the sense of sisterhood.

The gathering drew attendees from eighteen states and five countries, all hoping to find camaraderie and understanding in a world that stigmatizes their status. This was the one place where no one would be asked if they had children or if they planned to start a family. The presumption was that no one did. It was there that a fellow attendee schooled me on the "mother" of the child-free movement, Ellen Peck. Her controversial 1971 book *The Baby Trap* was out of print, but I hunted it down from an online bookseller. In chapter 10, "Beyond the Baby Trap: Coping with Culture," she writes:

> Escaping the baby trap, physically, is as easy as taking the Pill. But there are more subtle factors operating psychologically, factors that can weaken your will about the Pill, factors that can undermine your confidence in the tightness of your decision not to have children. There are pressures that can make you feel isolated, different, even guilty, because you're childless. Pressures that can tempt you to think, "Oh, it'd be so much easier just to go ahead and get pregnant, just like everybody else. Then maybe people would stop hammering at me." Pressures that can accumulate and be responsible for that "forgotten" Pill, that subconscious "mistake."[8]

Peck encourages women to stand firm in their decision not to have kids, even laying out snarky retorts for when friends and family pressure you. My favorite:

> For example, you run into Frayna Loeb, a former roommate you never could stand, at a downtown department store. She hushes her four-year-old with a sharp slap on the hand; complains that her

five-year-old has ("without permission, you bad boy, Johnny") asked some little friends over for the afternoon so she has to run home quick to fix peanut-butter-and-jelly sandwiches; adjusts her one-year-old in the Toddler Tote, saying "Thank goodness this one isn't quite old enough to socialize yet"; then breaks off, looks at you hard, and simps: "And what about you and Bill? Don't you have any children yet?"

Okay. Indulge yourself. "Of course not. We're too smart for that." Or, "Never! We're having too much fun!" And dash off to meet your husband for lunch.[9]

And then these zingers for cocktail parties:

Question: What's the matter?
No kids yet? Don't you like children?

Response: Yes. Other people's. And on occasion.
Or: Yes. And we want to keep on liking children.

Comment: Lucy and Harry have three children.

Response: Yes, Lucy and Harry
do have their problems.[10]

It's hard not to appreciate Peck's unapologetic stance, even if you have kids. I could see why she is a hero to some of these women.

I sat through seminars and panel discussions on everything from how to get through the holidays alone to estate planning for one. This was the very definition of a safe space for child-free women. As I waited for one session to begin, a panelist burst into the room with notable agitation. "Hey, did you guys see that *reeaaally* pregnant woman in the lobby," she quipped in an exasperated tone. "Ugh. Her shirt barely covered her stomach. I wanted to trip her." Like I said, safe space.

I was particularly struck by how the childless by chance and childless by choice women worked side by side. For a discussion on dealing the rudeness and insensitivities they so commonly faced, one woman shared that having an abortion was the best decision she ever made. It allowed her to follow her dreams and live her life on her own terms. The woman next to her then shared how she had gone through several rounds of painful, expensive IVF with no luck. Though we were all misty-eyed as she shared the story of how all her siblings had large families, something her parents valued. During one holiday gathering, her mother asked that she and her husband not stand in the family photo because it was for "everyone with kids." Another woman said the biggest annoyance with being child-free and single is the assumption that she is gay, as if having a child somehow confirms your sexual preference. Everyone shared the not-so-subtle comments they endured:

"You will regret this choice later."

"You are making a silly mistake."

"This is a selfish thing to do to your parents. They want grandchildren."

"You are going to grow old and lonely."

"What was the point of getting
married if you don't have kids?"

"Don't you want to leave something behind?"

"Who's going to take care of you when you get old?"

"You must hate kids."

"You may not think so now, but this
is a really stupid decision."

These may seem like innocuous comments, opinions
that you feel entitled to share. The truth is that they do
a great deal of harm to these women. We often talk of
microaggressions in regard to race and sexism, but let's
consider it in this circumstance. Microaggressions are
defined as everyday indignities—whether intentional or
unintentional—conveyed by words or actions that give
off hostile and derogatory messages. The comments are
often fleeting and easily overlooked unless you are on the
receiving end. "I never knew love until I became a mom."
What does this tell a not mom? You don't know love. Your
life is inadequate. How do you think that makes a woman
feel? These types of remarks diminish the lives that they
live. We have to ask ourselves, *Why do we continue to criticize and mock what should be another valid choice?*

They Don't Want Your Life

Like it or not, more and more women are opting out of
motherhood. The reasons are manifold and complex. Many
cited a desire to maintain independence and spontaneity,

some talked of fear of climate change and pollution, and others enjoyed their romantic relationships and did not want to change that dynamic. Not surprisingly, a study conducted by Britain's Open University found that childless couples have happier unions.[11] You can't deny that having a child can add stress, pressure, and tension to a marriage or partnership. However, my conversations with empty nesters and parents of self-sufficient teens suggest children provide more fulfillment long term.

Most of the child-free women I encountered confessed they just didn't have a maternal instinct. As far back as they can remember, they were turned off by the thought of being a mom. "Dammit. I don't want to. Never have, and I'm confident I never will," said one exasperated woman rolling her eyes. When will that be explanation enough? The fact is, deciding not to have children is rarely a rash decision.

Maya, an Atlanta-based attorney, was pretty sure she didn't want kids until she met her ideal mate. She decided to reevaluate what had once been a steadfast belief that she wasn't meant to be a mother. She took a sojourn to Africa alone to think about what she wanted from her life and what she needed. She came back more sure than ever that kids were not for her. "People don't take into account that we know ourselves," she said. "Isn't it better to know it's not the right thing for you rather than have kids because everyone says you should, then resent the decision later?"

This pressure isn't limited to heterosexual women. Not long ago, having children felt out of reach for lesbian couples. Today, however, between 2 million and 3.7 million children under age eighteen have an LBGTQ parent and around two hundred thousand of them are being raised by a same-sex couple.[12] The greater visibility of lesbian and gay parents has contributed to the expectation that women in same-sex couples should want to have children as well.[13]

"I just worry about your happiness in the long term," well-meaning friends and family may say. Is it so impossible to believe that many women remain content with their choice even as they exit their childbearing years? In 2015, a controversial study from London School of Economics researcher Satoshi Kanazawa uncovered a link between intelligence and the desire to be a mom. In his book *The Intelligence Paradox: Why the Intelligent Choice Isn't Always the Smart One*, he claims, "Intelligent people—especially intelligent women—have fewer children and are more likely to remain childless for life than less intelligent people."[14] Ouch! Basically, this suggests smarter women are less likely to want kids. Surprisingly, Pew Research Center data appears to back up that claim, asserting that the most educated women are less likely to have children.[15]

It's hard not to be a little insulted by the findings. I've met many brilliant women on both sides. I like to think that the point of this research isn't to diminish us but rather to put the choice to not be a mom in a different perspective.

Going Incognito

At a keynote address at the NotMom Summit, I joined a table full of academics, all of whom slipped into conversation that they were not moms by choice, and proudly so. The speaker, Melanie Notkin, author of *Otherhood: Modern Women Finding a New Kind of Happiness*, talked about other significant ways we can mother and feel connected to children. Her regret about not having a family of her own was palpable. You could tell by the wistful lilt of her voice and the still hopeful glint in her eye. She had dreamed of her wedding since age ten and of having twins. Then, one day she woke up single, childless, and an entrepreneur. It may not have been her intention, but it seemed a fate she accepted.

It was a narrative that didn't sit well with many of my tablemates. One abruptly gathered her things and left. I must confess, I was in constant fear someone would ask a question that would force me to reveal that I was a traitor. I was *a mom*. It was an interesting position to be in. This is the one time I wasn't eager to share that I was a parent. This must be how they felt all the time—misplaced, like not a member of the club.

An Unconscious Betrayal

Many moms seem to have an almost instinctual response to distance themselves from these women whose lives no longer parallel their own. Sometimes we think they will be bored or annoyed by our obsession with our children. Other times, it's born of guilt. "When I got pregnant, the hardest phone call I had to make was to this friend who took it as a betrayal," mother-of-two Gaye divulged, wearing a guilty expression. For years she was adamant about not having kids, a plan she had shared with this good friend. Then she changed her mind. "Somehow it was as if we were on the same page, and then, all of a sudden, I changed the page, and she was having a really hard time with it. We are still friends, but it's not the same. It's a weird divide."

Our Biggest Blunder

We misunderstand a lot about the lives of our child-free friends. I was recently working on a project with a single media executive who lives in L.A., and she volunteered how her friends with kids just "went away." She laughed, but I could tell it was hurtful. She went on, "I think they think I don't have any interest in their family lives. It's kind of sad, I guess." Indeed, it is. Child-free women aren't invited to the kids' birthday parties or recitals. They are no longer the go-to bud, replaced by a new crew of mommy friends. Truth is, they want to be involved in your life. One of the most frequent complaints on the Childfree Choice Facebook page, which has more than thirty-two thousand followers, is that they are not included in family activities because people assume they don't want to be around children.

"You start hearing things like, 'Well, you don't have kids, you wouldn't understand,'" said Jessica Wade, the page founder. "That's not always true. But what ends up happening is that slowly—and sometimes immediately—people pull away. Parents will say we just can't be friends anymore. They think our values don't align anymore. That happens a lot more than you would think." Wade launched the page as part of a college project, but it quickly grew into so much more. It became a sounding board for others like her, a place where they could find like-minded people and avoid the judgment that they faced on a daily basis.

The mistreatment isn't restricted to their personal lives. Many childless women report workplace discrimination at the hands of men and, sadly, mothers. Work-life balance isn't even a consideration for them. The notion is that if you don't have a household to manage, what exactly do you need to balance? Instead, colleagues without kids say they are asked to work later and pitch in on holidays more often, and that their personal time is not viewed as important as that of a parent. Another point of contention is the parental leave and flextime policies that only apply to parents. Even if you don't have children, you may still need to care for yourself or another family member. Changing work policies is certainly a tall order, but helping lift the misconceptions about the child-free is something we can do right now in our own interactions with them.

What They ~~Want~~ Need You to Know

Child-free women need what every woman needs: respect and acceptance. Whether we intended to our not, most of us have been guilty of making a child-free friend feel as though their choice is less than. It's an easy transgression to repair if you are willing. Recently, I reached out to a high school friend I had essentially abandoned since having my second child. I apologized for not being there for her, and that is something that I was intent on changing.

I apologized for not always returning emails and texts and being a complete nightmare to schedule anything with. She was touched and appreciative and, like me, eager to rekindle our bond. It's easy to attach grandiose meaning to motherhood. But let's ask ourselves this: Shouldn't women be allowed to find great meaning in their lives whether or not children are a part of it?

YOUR NEW TO-DO LIST

1. Reconnect with a child-free friend you haven't seen in a while. Trust me, you will appreciate having downtime with someone who isn't freaking out over milestones, kindergarten applications, and picky eating habits. When you meet, share the ups and downs of parenting but don't dominate the conversation with kid-talk. Be sure to allow your friend a place to share what is happening in her life.

2. Resist the urge to ask a childless woman when they are going to have kids. If they don't want kids, they are sick of hearing the question. If they want kids but are having fertility issues, it's painful to talk about.

3. Be present for the big events in their lives. They may not have children, but there are still milestones that are special to them like graduations, new jobs, promotions, any moment that celebrates the life they have chosen.

Six

Post-Kid Marriage: It's a Thin Line Between Love and Hate

WHAT TO REALLY EXPECT:
You and your partner may have totally different visions of what parenthood will look like. This will be the source of a lot of tension. A. Lot. Of. Tension.

Carmen was beside herself the morning I sat down with her. It wasn't the act of getting her kids—ages eight, six, and four—fed and out the door that had her so manic. It was her husband. The night before, he had expressed his profound disappointment with her. Lately, he brooded, things had changed and not for the better. He worried she was not on her game with the kids, with dinnertime, with all the things he was used to her being on top of. Before you label him a total prick, here is the thing you need to know about their marriage—the "who does what" of their relationship was established many years ago. Carmen, a former schoolteacher, stopped working when they started a family. They moved to a new city, he started a new job, and she took care of everything on the home front. Absolutely everything. There was no explicit conversation about this, but their roles fell into place. She would do the cooking, shopping, and appointments and, of course, deal with all the kid-related stuff. He would work. The fact that she was burned-out, overwhelmed, and tired was completely lost on him. She wanted him to do more on the home front, but he felt the logistics of their lives had been solidified long ago.

This, my friends, is the cautionary tale you must heed. A lot of couples think that having children will bring them closer, but to the contrary, we sometimes become more disenchanted with our relationships.[1] Taking care of children is stressful, to be sure, but it's more than that. Being parents significantly changes how we interact and communicate with one another. Life becomes more trans-actional. By that I mean life becomes an endless to-do list, and we can't help focusing on what we do compared to what our partner does not.

"It's your turn to do bath time. I did it last night."

"You need to do pickup sometimes. It's not fair."

"I'll take Timmy to soccer if you take Chloe to ballet."

It's important to note that men are pitching in more than ever, and there are roughly two million stay-at-home dads, yet in this country, home and kids remains largely the domain of moms.[2] Family responsibilities are still often divvied up into what our grandmothers might have called "pink" and "blue" roles. It's not just a dilemma for stay-at-home moms. There were similar complaints from women who spent ten hours a day behind the desk or on their feet all day only to come home and begin what is popularly called the second shift, hours laboring to make dinner, clean the house, get kids ready for bed, set out clothes for the next day, pack lunches, the list goes on.

Same-sex couples aren't immune either. New Jersey mother-of-two Rose thought she would bypass those stereotypical gender roles. She was married to a woman, after all, and both had busy, high-profile careers. A few months into motherhood, however, it was clear that one of them would have to take on the lion's share of the kid-centered day-to-day. Her wife was better at the tedious tasks like budgets and taxes; Rose was the guru of the birthday parties and playdates. "We played to our strengths," she said with an air of defeat. In fact, feelings of defeat and resentment are what many moms expressed when the conversation turned to what's happening in their marriages.

How Did We Get Here?

The women I interviewed typically took one of three paths to parenthood. There are the ones who carefully planned with their partner, deciding on the right time to start a family. Then there is the contingent who was surprised but happy to learn they are expecting. Lastly, there are women who were completely ambivalent about becoming parents, debating whether it was the right choice, sometimes still questioning the decision up until delivery. But regardless of *how* they became moms, one thing becomes true for all once they *are* moms: the inevitability of burnout.

Of course, burnout is an affliction that runs through our entire culture. We are all living in a constant state of overwhelm. Raising a family has an entirely different set of criteria than it did when our grandparents had kids. The biggest shift is that we are constantly connected, which is both the blessing and curse of technology.

I was sitting down to lunch with a mom of two from Virginia while she was traveling through New York on business. What could have been a leisurely, sixty-minute meal—the only time she could spare—was constantly interrupted by dings from her phone. It wasn't just about work. The school reached out about her daughter; her husband couldn't find their son's basketball shoes; her assistant reminded her of a meeting that had been added to her schedule. At some point, she even wondered what her family should have for dinner that night, and she wouldn't even be there for it.

She wasn't necessarily flustered by all of this. These nonstop interruptions had just become a part of her life as a worker, mom, wife, human. Like Silly Putty in the hands of a toddler, we are stretched beyond what we thought was possible, but we muddle through as all moms do. But we don't muddle through it unscathed.

Quantifying the Invisible

This never-ending to-do list has a name: invisible labor, and it's been getting a bit more attention lately. Thank goodness. It's all those little, hard-to-quantify duties that keep the family and home flowing. Making sure everyone's favorite snacks are in the cupboard, soymilk for one kid, whole milk for another, the right toilet paper in the bathrooms, that the soccer cleats make it into the backpack, the permission slips are signed, arranging car pools, booking the annual dentist and doctor appointments, and the list goes on. It's all pretty innocuous on the surface, but this collection of little tasks takes a toll. It adds to our already soul-crushing mental load.

The night before we met, a mom confessed to waking up in a sweat wondering if she had the date wrong for the school bake sale. She was assigned the important task of making dairy-free cookies. This is the torment of the "default parent," the go-to grown-up in the house. And there is always a default regardless of the family dynamic. In fact, if you are reading this book, I can say with 99.9 percent certainty that is you.

There is a lot that goes into this role. It's not just checking off items on a list. It involves anticipating problems, figuring out what needs to be done, doing what needs to be done, and finally, keeping track of the situation. It requires a great deal of logistical and emotional fortitude. Shouldering this burden wreaks havoc not just on our emotional state but also the relationship with our partner. Of particular interest to women in heterosexual relationships, a United Nations report revealed modern women still do nearly three times as much unpaid domestic work as men.[3] On top of that, a 2016 study that appeared in the journal *Brain and Behavior* revealed that women were twice as likely as men to suffer severe stress and anxiety.[4] I can already hear the chorus: "Tell me something I don't know!"

The Letdown

This dynamic is the source of a great deal of resentment in relationships. It builds slowly, often sparked by the jealousy of thinking how little your spouse's day-to-day life has changed. "My husband had a month paternity leave," Twanna, a Silver Spring, Maryland, mother, recalled of life after her twins were born. "When he went back to work, it was like being on the outside watching him have that flexibility to kind of make decisions on the fly. That was a hard adjustment. I had to think about so much. When was the last time they ate? What time do I need to pump? What do I need to carry with me? I think that was what was most surprising. It was just this constant cycle that left me with no time for myself."

It's such a common tale of woe, as inevitable as that mountain of diapers packed into the bin every day. The self-pity is made more acute by the fact that your partner doesn't seem to carry the same burdens. They can meet colleagues after work while you rush to make the daycare pick-up deadline. No matter how busy your own work calendar, you are always the one to take off work to nurse a sick child. If you stay at home, maybe it's that they come home after what you imagine was a day full of adult conversation and interaction, talking about how they are forging ahead with career goals, a freedom that is becoming a distant memory to you. Here are the most common complaints that I heard.

> "He can come and go as he pleases
> without the same pressure."

"He comes home, sees the kids driving me crazy, and doesn't even offer to help!"

"What about my time? What about what I want or need to stay sane?"

"My husband does NOTHING!"

"I swear we didn't fight before having a baby!"

"If he really wanted sex, he'd empty the dishwasher."

"I'm with the kids all day, and he comes in and hides out in the bathroom."

"It's hard to be romantic with someone who does nothing to help you."

It's important to note that feeling resentful of your spouse and all the responsibilities that being a partner and mother entail does not necessarily mean you hate motherhood. Parenthood isn't the issue. The problem is that you are drowning in a sea of unmet and unclarified expectations.

When we are prepping for a baby, we spend hours upon hours researching the best cribs, the safest car seats, even picking out decorations for nursery themes. It took me three trips and I don't know how many hours in the paint store to decide which brand and which hue to use. Then there is the physical prep. I know countless moms who never missed their weekly prenatal yoga or Lamaze class, the cultural rite of passage for every expectant couple. It's all about the baby's needs and birth plans. The one thing we often neglect to do, however, is the necessary emotional groundwork for this next stage of couplehood.

Lamaze for Your Marriage

I can't tell you how many people I spoke with who admitted to getting a dog in hopes that it would get them ready for the responsibility of caring for a child. In full disclosure, my husband and I bought into this foolish notion too a year after we married. Let me be crystal clear here: in no way does caring for a twelve-pound Shih Tzu ready you for parenthood. In. No. Way. You cannot crate a baby when you go to work. You cannot lay out wee-wee pads for it if you are going to be home late. Splitting up dog walks with your partner hardly compares to the help you will need once baby arrives. I found it interesting that couples will negotiate how they will divide up pet duty but never even think about having the same discussion about life with a baby.

· The truth is, most of us never talk about what a baby will do to our relationships. I think that is because we don't really think it will change the way we feel about our partners. It's very likely that you never loved your partner more than the day you decided to start a family. Here is another important truth: it's also likely that you will never despise that person more than after your child arrives. It's a bizarre emotional turn. Those blessed little bundles are often longed for and dreamed about. Some babies arrive with the help of costly medical intervention. Others are a welcome surprise.

We have this unconscious expectation that we will "figure it out" and that the baby will fit into the lives we have already created. "It never entered my mind to have a conversation about what our daily lives would be like when we were planning to have kids," confessed Amanda (remember her from the stroller assembly disaster). "Then after you get pregnant, you are so excited, you don't think about it then either." What gets lost in the fog of new parenthood is what the two of you need to do to stay connected.

The Ghosts of Our Childhood

Amidst all the excitement of becoming parents, we need to prepare for the expectations we didn't know we had. Whether you realize it or not, we all carry unique expectations about what it means to be a mother or father. We are also influenced by our own childhood and the family dynamics we grew up with.

My husband was raised in a very old-school, traditional home. His mom loved cooking, cleaning, taking care of her family. It gave her great joy. She never required her son to wash a dish, load the laundry, anything she considered to be her job as his mom. I, on the other hand, grew up in a very progressive family. My dad was the clean freak, and his recipes rivaled my mom's. I never thought of married life as having a gendered division of labor.

These differences weren't an issue until we had kids. Though we both had busy, high-profile careers, there was an expectation that I would take care of most things on the home front even when I, too, felt overwhelmed by work. It can be a tough adjustment. Fireflies trapped in a jar, I thought, as Carmen and so many other women described how they felt. They now had these parameters that limited what they could do outside family life, all the while looking at the outside world go by. I know it sounds a bit melodramatic, and not every woman will experience new motherhood this way, but for those who do, it's critical to process the changes that are happening, discuss them, and set new expectations and rules.

Whether you already have kids or are just starting the process, I encourage both of you to answer the following questions independently and share your answers with one another:

What role do you expect to play in the day-to-day care of the baby?

Will we hire a sitter or use a daycare center?

If one of us needs to cut back at work or stay home, who will that be?

Do you have a parenting philosophy? If so, what is it?

How do you plan to discipline?

How will we spend time together as a family on the weekends?

How much time will we try to carve out for our friends?

What role will grandparents play?

Some of the answers may surprise you, especially if you realize you are not on the same page. Knowing your partner's perspective will help you plan and, more importantly, negotiate who will do what.

There is a growing population of couples who even go to prebaby counseling sessions. Therapist Esther Boykin, author of *The Date Deck*, is among the relationship experts who want us to think of therapy as a preventative resource rather than the Hail Mary after everything goes to hell. She likens it to going to the gym or eating healthy.

All those characteristics about your partner that you fell in love with—that's all great. But your core values come out when you have kids. If there is not agreement, the differences will take front and center. It can even be over something simple. My husband and I have conflicting philosophies on sleepovers. He is adamantly against them. When we first started to debate the topic, he loved to say Cubans don't do sleepovers. When he used to ask his parents if he could spend the night at a friend's home, his father would say, "What's wrong with your bed?" We argued endlessly about it. I rolled my eyes and acquiesced for a while. To me this was an adolescent rite of passage, something I had wonderful memories of from my own childhood.

As Lex had to decline more and more invites from his best buds, I pressed the issue again. My husband revealed that a childhood friend had been molested, and he always carried that fear for his own children. "What if something were to happen to him at a sleepover?" he asked. "That is something we could never take back." This is the discussion we should have had from the beginning. Being up-front about why we believe what we believe allows for greater understanding and empathy. Others confessed to being blindsided by differing views on public versus private school, which side of the family to spend holidays with, whether spanking is an acceptable form of discipline, and even the best way to soothe a baby in the middle of the night.

On the more spiritual end of the spectrum, I spoke to couples who, though raised under different religions, never discussed what to teach their children until they were parents. These kinds of issues can be turning points for a pair. How strong is that bond at its core? Put simply, parenthood puts your relationship to the ultimate test. The goal isn't to come to perfect agreement, but being mindful of the differences can make it less of a shock when they come up as we actively parent.

Assuming Makes an Ass Out of . . .

Once we are in the throes of parenthood, we also make the mistake of assuming our spouse will intuit what we need. Admittedly, some can. There are partners who can anticipate what the other wants. However, I did not find that to be the dynamic in the majority of the cases. I was with a small group of moms in Florida, and each lamented about a different thing her partner was clueless about, from the morning routine to managing all the after-school activities for multiple kids to the medications the children had to take.

In my case, prepping for family outings on the weekends was a pain point. I would run around getting toys, bottles, and snacks ready. After dressing the kids and then myself, I was sweat soaked. My husband, on the other hand, would calmly get himself ready, never seeming to notice all that needed to happen to get us all out the door. And then I would spend half the day pissed at him, making snippy comments but never verbalizing why I was so annoyed. From my perspective, he should have *known* he was supposed to help. It's common sense, I'd say to myself. Sadly, it doesn't always work that way. He's not a mind reader.

Oftentimes our partners don't see everything that goes into taking care of the family. Researchers at Arizona State University surveyed 393 American moms with children under eighteen and measured the division of labor by three tasks:[5]

1. Organizing the family schedules. Nine out of ten women felt solely responsible for this realm of family life.

2. Fostering the children's well-being. Eight out of ten women admitted they were the parent who took care of their kids' physical and emotional needs.

3. Making major financial decisions. While 50 percent of women said they make investment, vacation, car purchases, and home improvement decisions alongside their partners, it was not reported as an empowering role but rather just another worrisome burden.

Is it any wonder that two-thirds of couples say that marital satisfaction takes a deep dive after the first child is born?[6]

By the end of a long day, you are ready to lash out. You argue about housework, quality time with kids, who does what, who does more, are they doing their fair share. This appears to be the biggest source of conflict among parents of young children. You feel taken for granted, your mate feels attacked, and there is no room for objectivity on either side. What I learned from spending time with moms from different backgrounds is that most women, myself included, don't know how to talk about things that bother us without getting upset or even blowing up at our partner.

We have to find ways to address these things in a productive way. Easier said than done when you watch your spouse step over dirty clothes on the floor without considering putting them in the hamper or ignore the overflowing trash can or the dishes that need to be loaded in the dishwasher.

After a long period of stewing (and by that, I mean years), I finally accepted what I needed to do: tell my husband exactly what I needed and what I expected of him. If you approach the conversation calmly as opposed to at the height of your anger and annoyance, you have a better chance of getting what you need. Now, the night before we have plans, I let Caleb know how we will divide and conquer the kids in the morning. Sometimes there is a lot of minutiae involved in that communication, down to who is making sure who brushes their teeth. Does this get a little tiresome? Yes, of course. Yet, it is not nearly as draining as carrying around squint-eyed, silent rage all day long. And, to be honest, he's happy to help when he knows what needs to be done.

I think the crux of the problem lies within the fact that people don't always share the same definition of "worthy contribution." During their study, the Cowans commonly heard complaints like, "He said he was going to be a really involved dad, and he's just not doing it." In return, her husband would shout, "Do you know how many diapers

I changed this week?" They had different perspectives on what counted. He was thinking of his work as part of his support for the family and part of raising the baby. She wanted more of a contribution on the domestic front. Getting these things on the table and getting couples to think about them in a less blaming way is the path for a more equitable and livable existence for you both. Again, resolving this requires talking without attacking.

It's all about communication, advises Dr. Anlee Kuo, a San Francisco–based psychiatrist who works with women and families at their most vulnerable times. "The newborn and toddler stages can be a real test of a relationship," she warned. "A successful relationship is about effective communication. You have to communicate and put everything out there. There is going to be shifting, having disagreements, and working things through. You have to be willing to get help if you need help."

This won't always be easy, but the negotiating of roles is necessary. It's not about a perfect division of duties, but try to work out one that doesn't leave you physically and emotionally depleted every day. It's also important that you appreciate what the other person is doing and express that appreciation. We all want our efforts to be seen and acknowledged.

Learn to Let Go

As much as we want our partners to "help more," it is also hard for many of us to let go when they do. Twanna's spouse could tell she needed time away, so he encouraged her to go out with friends, ensuring her he could handle the twins. As much as she desperately wanted some kid-free time, she didn't completely trust his ability to care for them like she did.

"You feel like, I personally carried this child or these children, and I can't afford for anything to go wrong," she said of her conflicted feelings. And you know, even though he has paternal instincts and all of that, I think sometimes we don't necessarily trust it like we do our maternal instincts. We feel as if, I actually know how to take care of my baby; you don't. Even though this was both of our first time doing it, I also felt like I'm more in tune with them. I'm with them all day. I know what this kind of cry means or this sound means, while you're just going to brush it off. So even though I wanted the flexibility to kind of come and go as I felt like, I also had that sense of concern like, *Is he gonna take care of them like I'm gonna take care of them?*"

The answer is, no, he can't. How could he? He doesn't do it as often as you do, so he's less practiced and efficient. That doesn't mean he's going to lose one of them at the playground.

Fear isn't the only emotion that makes us hesitant to hand over the reins. If a partner asks a million questions about how to do something, it can be incredibly frustrating, prompting us to just want to do it ourselves. My son, now a preteen, was diagnosed with a long list of food allergies when he was four. Every time my husband goes out with him, he texts me asking what Lex is allergic to. It's annoying. *Why can't he remember like I do*, I grouse silently. But I roll my eyes, send the list, and enjoy the freedom I am getting to do whatever it is I want to do in that moment.

We need to stop looking at it as though our partners are doing us a favor or something special by taking care of their children. It's their job too. We also have to accept that we are not the only ones that can do a good job parenting our children. Our partner may have a different parenting style. He or she will do things differently than we do. As long as no one is in danger, so what? Your toddler isn't going to evaporate if your spouse doesn't make his snack the same way or doesn't coddle him when he cries.

Sometimes, the most important thing a mother can do for her sanity is to let go of control. Accept the help and express how much you appreciate what your partner is doing. This bit of advice usually elicits eye rolls. *Why should he get accolades for what he is supposed to do anyway?* All of us crave acknowledgment and, like our children, encouragement inspires them to be more helpful, involved partners.

Coupledom During the Coronavirus Pandemic

Regular family life is taxing enough. To be confined together for an unspecified amount of time is a recipe for disaster. There is no question that you will get on one another's nerves at some point. A week into home confinement, I wondered if a radioactive spider had bitten me because the sound of my family chewing seemed especially loud. It drove me bonkers. Though the biggest complaint I heard from women was that their partners were not helping out enough with cleaning, cooking, or taking care of the kids. Never have these partnerships been so strained. Many women have been confronted with a very uncomfortable truth: when it comes to life at home, there is no partnership even in the face of a national disaster. Needless to say, there were a lot of nasty looks, crossed arms, and arguments in homes across the country.

The couples that fared better were those who set up a duty chart at the start of each week. It wasn't perfectly executed each time, but the expected responsibilities were laid out. Ideally, in times of forced closeness, couples would, well, get closer. "It's a good time to talk to each other," suggested Dr. Phil Cowan. "Talk about dreams you have, plans you want to make together. Anything that is more collaborative."

YOUR NEW TO-DO LIST

There is often a discrepancy between what we expect from parenting with a partner and what really happens. Take the time to fill out these questions independently and make a date to trade answers. Remember, the goal is to be more mindful of the differences, not necessarily solve them all in one sitting.

PREPARENT QUESTIONNAIRE

1. What kind of parent do you want to be?

2. What kind of parent do you think your partner will be?

3. What do you think your partner thinks about parenting?

4. Will both parents work?

5. If you both work, who will stay home if your child is sick?

6. Will you both go to doctors' appointments?

7. Will you spank?

8. What will you do if you and your partner disagree about something?

9. How would you describe your childhood in one hundred words or less?

10. What role will grandparents play? Will they have a say in how you raise your children?

11. What religion will you practice, if any?

12. If you both work, will your baby go to daycare, or will you hire a nanny?

13. If one of you has to take a step back from their career, who will it be?

How to Communicate What You Need

If you take away nothing else from this chapter, please remember that your partner won't know how you feel or what you are going through until you tell them.

1. **Don't let the tension mount.** Be honest about what you are feeling. Keeping things bottled up hardly ever works. It manifests as irritability, quick-tempered responses, and arguments. As opposed to complaining under your breath as you angrily load the dishwasher,

set aside a time to talk face-to-face. Explain how tired and overwhelmed you are feeling. Just acknowledging these feelings can do a lot of good for a couple. Encourage your partner to open up and share how they feel as well. Chances are you are both experiencing the emotional and physical toll of working, raising a family, and keeping a household running.

2. **Be practical about what can actually change.** Have realistic expectations. Men can't breastfeed, for example, and there may be things you are just much better at dealing with. But if they do step up, don't hover or criticize.

3. **Designate jobs.** Write down everything each of you is supposed to do each week, from paying bills to who gets up at 2:00 a.m. to change the diaper. I can honestly say that keeping a Google calendar has single-handedly saved my sanity and—by extension—my marriage. Every recital, game, appointment is scheduled there. It's also a good way for both of us to see what the other has to do. Keep in mind that life is messy and sometimes you have to do things off book, but having clear responsibilities helps each parent stay organized and sane.

4. **Don't assume they know what they should be doing.** Be explicit about how you need to divide and conquer dealing with the kids and home.

5. **Stop keeping score.** It instantly makes your partner feel defensive, and it certainly doesn't engender a desire to do more. Let them know how tired you are and how you need them to help.

6. **Let go of the way things used to be.** After kids, your marriage inevitably changes. Nostalgia for that former relationship can be a dangerous thing if it's keeping you from adapting to this new life and lifestyle together.

Seven

Who Needs the "I Have a Headache" Excuse When You Have Kids?

WHAT TO REALLY EXPECT:
Sex may never be the same again.

On Valentine's Day one year, I stopped by a neighbor's apartment to drop something off for her kids. As soon as she opened the door, I recognized the red, glassy glare of pink eye. "Oh no. Of all days," I offered sympathetically. She raised an eyebrow and said, "Are you kidding? This is the best get-out-of-sex excuse I've ever had."

This entire notion of the sexless marriage has been the butt of standup routines, TV shows, and movies for decades and for good reason. It's as comical as it is common. At some point, most couples notice they just don't have as much sex as they used to. Add in kids to the equation and the number takes a deeper dive. I won't go as far as to say that having kids is the death of sex, but it can certainly lead to the death of sex as you know it.

133

A 2018 study of one thousand parents exposed a pretty troubling picture about coitus post-kids. Nearly half of moms said that having children made their sex lives worse, and most reported an overall decrease in libido.[1] Though I should note, 40 percent say their sex lives were unchanged, and 13 percent say their sex lives improved since becoming moms. If there was ever a reason to be jealous of another mom, that may be it.

First, we should talk about what is considered "normal" in our culture. According to the General Social Survey, the average married couple has sex fifty-eight times a year, which is around once per week.[2] That number elicits various responses from women. Some think it's spot on, others think it's too much, and others too few. The number doesn't really matter. What is most important is what is normal for you and your partner—and whether that changes after kids in a way that is destructive to your marriage.

Our first instinct may be to think that a sexless marriage can create a host of issues in a relationship. But what is clear from my conversations is that it is more of a symptom of something than the cause. Experts say as many as 15 to 20 percent of married couples are rarely having sex, if at all.[3] What constitutes "sexless," you are probably wondering self-consciously?

Some say you've earned the label if you have not been intimate with your partner within the last six to twelve months. Others assign a specific number: ten times or less in the last year. Here is the thing I want to prepare you for: that once hot and heavy bond (the one that probably led to that kid of yours in the first place) may turn a bit frigid in the months after your baby is born, and that's perfectly normal.

How Did We Get Here?

There are many factors that can impact our intimacy with a partner. First of all, just having sex with children in the house requires a great deal of unsexy strategic planning.[4] Spontaneity is all but dead.

67 percent of parents wait until their kids are asleep.

64 percent feel the need to be extra, extra quiet.

54 percent say they put the kids to bed early.

42 percent sneak in private time while showering together.

39 percent distract their little ones with devices.

37 percent ship the kids off to a grandparent or other relative's house.

33 percent wait until the kids go to school.

Then there are those couples that are not putting in much of an effort at all. Evolutionary psychologists would say this is the natural progression of things in a relationship. Our brain triggers sexual desire so that we procreate. Once that's done, well, the biological necessity of sex comes to an end. Our attention then shifts to taking care of this family we created. Most moms will tell you it has more to do with their boobs than lack of some biology necessity.

After having a child, everything is new, including our bodies. That change can create an immense amount of self-consciousness. In those early weeks and months, it's easy to put it in the back of our minds as we concentrate on the task at hand—keeping this new little being alive. Eventually, however, we start taking long looks in the mirror, wondering if our bodies will ever get back to what they were. For some they will, though for the majority of us, some parts of this transformation are permanent. At breakfast with a group of moms, most of which had two children, the subject turned to our bodies.

"When I lie on my back, I can tuck my boobs under my arms. I'm serious."

"I swear my nipples meet my belly button."

"This tummy pouch is the worst."

"I went from an hourglass to an eggplant."

I shared the recent story of my toddler being in the bathroom when I stepped out of the shower. He took one look at me and said, "Ewwww, Mommy, gross." Now I have no idea what he was referring to. He was barely three at the time, and it's unlikely that he was even mildly aware of cultural standards of beauty. Still, I internalized it as a comment on what I looked like. "Well, Aidan, if Mommy is gross, you are the reason Mommy is gross," I said, assigning clear blame to the pregnancy that got him here. All the ladies at the breakfast table laughed and went on to share their own self-deprecating tales of body shame.

This dissatisfaction with our post-baby bodies is often a source of bonding for moms, but I wonder if these physical characteristics can be considered a badge of accomplishment instead. We did, after all, bring babies into this world. And even though childbirth happens every minute of every day, it's not without great risk. In fact, the US is one of the most dangerous places in the developed world to give birth, with seven hundred women dying during delivery every year and fifty thousand severely injured.[5] But I digress.

Body of Work

When I hear moms talk trash about their bodies, I can't help but feel pangs of guilt. Covering celebrities for more than a decade meant writing numerous stories about how celeb new moms pop back into skinny jeans a mere week after giving birth. And while we all know that stars have a lot of help to do it, this still sets a crazy, unrealistic standard. That has an effect on how we feel about ourselves and how we hold ourselves. Are we less confident? Are we less bold sexually because we wonder if our partner is focusing on that C-section scar and stretch marks?

These thoughts don't change the mechanics of sex, of course, but they certainly change how we engage our partners. After my second child, I was continually making cracks about my body. My husband walked up to me, looked me dead in the eye, and said, "I don't see you that way. I don't want to see you that way. Don't talk about yourself that way to me."

It was another aha moment. All those little changes are magnified in our eyes, but our partners don't always see us the way we see ourselves, nor do they want to.

It's important to boost our body confidence after having a baby. We can accomplish this in myriad ways, not just by losing weight. One mom swears by meditation; another says getting breast augmentation was the best decision she ever made. No judgment. I initially started running to drop the baby weight, but I soon discovered the pure bliss of the runner's high. The flood of endorphins makes me feel sexy and powerful. The weight loss is just an added bonus.

Who we surround ourselves with has an impact too. If we spend more time with women who are less focused on body image, we begin to deemphasize it too. So much research tells us that we shouldn't speak negatively about our bodies around young girls because it can negatively affect their self-image.[6] Couldn't the same be true of moms who feel vulnerable about their own appearance?

Positive self-talk is critically important to how we feel about ourselves. Whatever it is that works for you, it's important to find things that make you feel good about yourself and your body. Yes, your body undergoes changes when you have a baby, but it's up to you to make peace with and move beyond these changes. Even if just for the sake of intimacy with your partner, try to be aware of how you speak about your body and the effect it's having on your sex life. Find ways to reappreciate your body. Confidence isn't just something you feel; it's something you project. And it's sexy.

Many women also unwittingly feed our need for intimacy through friendships. "Women have this capacity to form deep, deep bonds with other women," explained psychotherapist McCaslin. These friendships can feed a lot of our emotional needs. Most heterosexual men, she noted, don't have that same dynamic with male friends. "A man's emotional support is usually his partner. In that way, women can feel burdened by male partners who have no one else."

Children can also distract us from partner bonds. Kids are on top of our bodies all day for holding, feeding, consoling. It's a phenomenon known as being "touched out." Is it such a stretch of the imagination that some women feel they don't want anyone else on their body for any reason? "Many mothers get a great deal of physical intimacy from their children," added McCaslin. "For some women, this is enough."

Another reason for the downshift in your sex drive might be fatigue or exhaustion. A study published in the *BMJ Open* medical journal revealed that women are just too tired for sex.[7] No duh! Not exactly a groundbreaking revelation for those of us with a few years of parenthood in the rearview, but scientific confirmation is always appreciated.

On any given night, you're dealing with a crying baby or a temperamental toddler or warring siblings, you realize it's 7:00 p.m., you have no idea what's for dinner, and you still have a mountain of work to get back to. Sex is the last thing on your mind. Going from lovers to parents has a way of turning a once hot and heavy relationship into something more akin to a business arrangement. It certainly does take a great deal of organizational and financial planning acumen to keep a family running, but the day-to-day of that is a surefire romance killer. Time together feels more like work.

The Toll of a Sexless Marriage

All of this inevitably creates an emotional distance. It can be imperceptible to friends and casual observers. But moms describe the loss of little moments, like holding hands, spooning, flirty texts, kissing, or even hugging with any regularity. It's not that they don't love their spouse; there is just a strain in their connection. The result could be just living parallel, platonic lives.

At a breakfast meet-up, one woman lamented, "We are like roommates," to a chorus of head nods. In many cases, moms shared that a lack of intimacy leads to more tensions overall. Is that argument really about dinner, or is the underlying problem that you both are feeling abandoned and disconnected from one another? It's something that can impact more than just your marriage. A 2012 study out of the University of Notre Dame found that kindergarteners whose parents fought frequently and aggressively were more likely to become emotionally insecure and struggle with depression, anxiety, and other behavioral issues.[8] In fact, the emotional damage may start long before then.

"Our children are learning from the time they are born," therapist Naphtali Roberts shared from her Burbank, California, office. "So if kids are noticing certain patterns of communication or lack of communication, if they are dealing with strong feelings within the parental relationship, that begins to be normalized from a very, very young age." The solution, however, does not require you to have a conflict-free marriage. I would like to meet the saints who could accomplish that. Again, it's about communication.

Rethink Who Is #1

Family therapists across the country tell me that they commonly treat couples in turmoil who have newborns and toddlers. It's a very vulnerable point in the relationship as they adjust to their new roles. Here's one upside: though marital satisfaction of new parents takes a dive, they are also less likely to actually divorce.[9]

From what most mothers tell me, the willingness to work through tough times gets intensified when you have children. And that's a good thing. However, how parents feel about themselves and each other impacts the family environment, and that's reason enough to get on top of it, according to Dr. Phil Cowan. A 2014 UK study of forty thousand households backs up that assertion, revealing that adolescents are happiest when their moms are happy with their partners.[10]

The work that we put into our marriage is of great importance. I think what most couples are not ready for is the fact that they will have several different marriages within one. In a lot of ways, it's the same concept as matrescence. You evolve and adapt as a mom, and so must a couple.

So often we tell ourselves that our kids should always come first. But perhaps it's time we realized that making our partnerships our top priority *is* what's best for our kids. If our kids benefit from a happy marriage, should we put our marriage first? Yes, this is the antithesis of what we have been conditioned to think as mothers, and the assertion may even enrage you, but hear me out.

First, please know that I am not suggesting you take away from the love and care you give a child. I recall two times when women have been proverbially burned at the stake for making this kind of comment to the media. In a 2005 *New York Times* essay, writer Ayelet Waldman boldly proclaimed, "I love my husband more than my children."[11] She credits this with the reason she was the only mom in the Mommy & Me class that "was getting any." She was instantly branded a bad mom and was hated by people nationwide.

In 2013, TV personality Giuliana Rancic didn't fare much better after saying the secret to a happy marriage is putting her husband first and her baby second.[12] The notion that you would prioritize marriage over kids may still feel unfathomable. But my conversations with moms have me convinced that Waldman and Rancic weren't so off base. If we give all of our emotion and passion to our kids, what happens to our marriages? When does that neglect start having an impact that is too hard to reverse?

Of course the immediate needs of our children will always trump our own. I'm not suggesting using the diaper money to buy Chardonnay and massage oil for date night. So what am I talking about? I am advocating prioritizing your relationship even in those early years of parenthood. Loving your child and loving your spouse is not an either-or proposition.

Our strong cultural bias toward accommodating and anticipating our kids' every need not only creates spoiled, impatient brats but also leaves us little energy for anything else. Instead of planning out the weekend so your kids are enriched and entertained every minute of the day, why not plan some grown-up time, something you as a couple will enjoy? Take time to talk to each other and, most importantly, listen. Every conversation doesn't have to be about the coming week's family calendar. Make space for you as a couple.

I have always hated hearing that "marriage is work." As if we are not working hard enough at just surviving. But it's absolutely true. You can't wait for things to just magically get better. You have to make it better.

Your Kids Are Taking Note

Having a healthy relationship is one of the best things you can do for your baby. Our children are incredibly astute and can sense tension, anger, and unhappiness, even when we think we are doing a good job of masking our emotions. "Kids tend to pick up cues from their parents," said Dr. Kuo, who does a great deal of trauma work with families. If you doubt just how perceptive your children are, consider this typical situation on the playground: when a child falls and the parent is overanxious and gets upset, the child will more often respond in kind. Whereas, if the parent is positive, calm, and reassuring, there is less of a chance your child will burst into tears or experience fear and worry over their accident. They learn from our reactions.

Children also need to see that people can be in conflict and work it out. They need to see love and compromise, not perfection. Living in a home where there is frequent conflict and turmoil can have a negative impact on young children. When parents fight, kids may feel responsible. "At that developmental age, if something bad is happening or if Mom is unhappy or Dad is unhappy, they may wonder, *Did I do that?*" explained Dr. Kuo. "They don't tend to have the perspective that I'm just one piece in the bigger picture. That comes later in development. Early on, everything is about them."

Modeling a healthy bond is more critical than you may imagine. We parents are our children's primary world. Parents shape their children's perspective. My husband insists on getting me flowers from the boys on holidays like Mother's Day and Valentine's Day. Not a big fan of flowers, I used to complain that it was a waste of money until he explained the reason why. He wanted our children to see that you should make the person who does so much for you feel loved and appreciated. It's not just a sweet gesture, but also an important one. I asked him if he would have the same philosophy if we had girls. "If we had daughters, it would be my job to teach them how they are supposed to be treated," he said. "So it's still important for them to see." We cannot underestimate the significance of the example we set for our children, even in our own relationships.

Redefine What It Means to Be Intimate

Really, it doesn't take a herculean effort to make your partner feel important or appreciated. Something as simple as saying good morning every day (I have talked to couples who don't say a word to each other in the mornings), a quick kiss good-bye (no tongue if you are not in the mood), flirt (compliment each other, make each other feel desired), ask how their day was when you reunite, and wait for the answer.

Then, there is sex. We could debate forever which comes first, chicken or egg. Does intimacy lead to sex, or does sex lead to intimacy? And there's no arguing that a satisfying sex life can result in more emotional intimacy.[13] But these are not the only ways to create much-needed closeness. In fact, modern parenthood requires a new or, at the very least, an expanded definition of intimacy.

For starters, we often mistake what we need for what our partner needs. Fact of the matter is the thing that makes you feel cherished and desired may be totally different from what makes your mate feel the same. Most women say the things that would make them feel most appreciated are: one, acknowledgment of how hard it is to take on the majority of the home and childcare duties; and two, pitching in without being nagged or guilted into helping.

If you are waiting for your partner to intuit this, however, you may end up waiting forever. Some things have to be spoken plainly to effect change. Unfortunately, we often express this kind of need during moments of rage, like when they pass the basket of unfolded laundry for the twentieth time. But you want a conversation, not a grudge match. Tell your partner what you need and let them tell you what they need in return. The goal should be for you both to feel seen and heard.

We can't be so obsessed with child-rearing that we forget our partner. If you are craving more intimacy, likely, so are they. New parenthood can be brutal on a relationship. Just remember that this stage is temporary. As your kids get older (and more independent), the tension and pressure you feel so acutely now will most certainly ease up.

YOUR NEW TO-DO LIST

1. **Work on being friends again.** I always say getting time away with my husband reminds me why I liked him in the first place. Alone time is a nice reminder of who we truly are, as opposed to the nagging eye-rollers who manifest most days of the week. Now, when I look at the overflowing trash can as he is sitting on the couch watching CNN, I try to visualize that beach in Aruba that brought us so much peace, and *then* I remind him to take the garbage out.

2. **Create new ways to be intimate.** Being close to your partner isn't just about intercourse.

3. **Experiment.** Now is the time to break out of the routine. It's not just about frequency, but also what you do with the time you have. A high number of moms who were able to rejuvenate their intimate relationships told me they did so by watching porn, experimenting with sex toys, and exploring new positions.

4. **Make the time to take care of your body.** This doesn't necessarily mean losing weight, though that is often a goal. Feeling better can come from doing things that make you feel better, whether that be running, yoga, meditation, taking classes to learn a new skill, or spending more time with friends. What is important is to reclaim or create activities that make you feel joyous and confident.

Eight

Not Every Woman Has the Mom Gene

WHAT TO REALLY EXPECT:
Being maternal may not come as naturally as you expect.

Even after marrying at twenty-seven, I felt no maternal tug, no need to nurture or bring a tiny version of myself into the world. It was a fact that intensely irked my traditional Cuban in-laws. As I mentioned earlier, when we failed to produce an heir in the first couple years, they assumed that something was wrong with me. That suspicion was made clear during one particular visit to them in their small New Jersey hometown. A very religious family, we always ended our trips with prayer. So I didn't blink an eye when Caleb's godmother walked over to him, put her hand on his shoulder, and started praying for God to grant him work success.

When she turned to me, I assumed it would be much of the same. My career, however, was the last thing on anyone's mind that day. Instead, she lifted up my blouse in front of everyone, made the sign of the cross on my stomach, and prayed for God to "heal my womb." Which wasn't broken, by the way.

I was angry but bit my tongue. She was one of the sweetest women I had met since joining the family, and I knew she didn't mean any harm. She was truly concerned. As unbelievable as the whole scene was, I was also perplexed by my complete lack of maternal longing. I was never particularly maternal. The little girls who wanted to play "house" or "mommy" at recess mystified me. They would pretend to cradle babies, make bottles, and set up a makeshift kitchen with leaves, sticks, and rocks. It was imaginative, to be sure, and how little girls were expected to play. It just never held any allure to me. While they changed the diapers of their baby dolls, I preferred Barbies. Mine weren't planning weddings to Ken or doing something so banal as setting up a nursery in the Dream House. They were flying around the world solving mysteries and having adventures.

Later, in college, I was equally bewildered by all the young women I met who dreamed of motherhood more than career. One of my roommates actually told me she felt it was what we were meant to do. I just couldn't relate. Having children was at the very bottom of my adulting to-do list at that point. Still, I had high hopes this maternal instinct would turn on one day, like a switch lighting a dark room.

Everyone swore that cradling friends' newborns in my arms would kick-start the yearning. It didn't. They insisted that my biological clock would start ticking away any day. It didn't. My husband was the one yearning to be a parent, sending me emails stating his own biological clock was ticking. Then his father was diagnosed with a terminal cancer. I knew it was his greatest wish to meet his grandchild, and I wanted that to happen for him. Was I ready? Who is ever really ready?

Not Wired for Motherhood

When I came across research into the existence of an actual mom gene, I wasn't just intrigued, I was obsessed with the notion. Could there really be a biological reason some of us don't crave having kids? It was a notion that really resonated with others, who like me, never felt like they were born to be moms. When I began interviewing women for this book, it was often the first question I asked: Do you think you have the mom gene?

It was a loaded question. To many, having the mom gene meant you were the kind of woman who always longed to be a parent and parented with ease. So the answer was often no. Of course, there were many women who knew it was something they wanted to do even as small children. Yet about half talked about children never being a part of their original life plan and being a mom eventually became a goal because of family pressures and the fear of later regretting not having them.

That was the experience of Gaye, the attorney and mother of two from New York City. I interviewed her in a small, informal focus group of other moms working in corporate America. "My husband and I negotiated them out of our wedding vows," she joked. "He didn't want them either." Eight years into marriage, the resolve started to weaken. Her mom kept asking who they were going to spend holidays with in their old age and insisted she'd regret not having kids. "Her best argument was that I needed a child so someone is forced to spend Christmas with me," she laughed. "She warned I would be totally alone one day and not happy about it."

Friends, too, were shocked she didn't want to have a baby with her tall, handsome husband. They struck a new deal: they would try. If it happened, great, and if not, fine. In reality, Gaye was far too type A for that kind of plan. When they didn't get pregnant right away, she started combing through every book on fertility and went on all the blogs to figure out how to up their chances. "I read that some people used egg whites," she shared.

"You mean you eat them?" I asked, echoing the curiosity of the other women. "Oh, umm, no," she paused a beat. "You use them as lubricant."

It took a few seconds for our brains to process what she said; then the quiet room erupted into laughter. "I know, I know. Crazy, right? It's totally not sanitary," she said as she blushed. "This was my worst nightmare. I ended up with salmonella poisoning. I've never been so sick in my life. My poor husband was like, 'I knew this shit was nasty.'" This was an astonishing tale for two reasons: Gaye, more than any other mother I interviewed, is rational, practical, and incredibly astute. More remarkable was the fact that she spent most of her life not wanting kids. The irony wasn't lost on her: "For so long, I was like no kids, and then I get salmonella poisoning from trying every random, unproven method." Two kids later, she still questions whether she has the so-called mom gene. "It's all about doing the best I can," she said with a shrug.

How Did We Get Here?

Our whole lives we've been sold on the idea of a maternal instinct. I had never even changed a diaper when I had my first child, so I had my doubts. I had been around babies, of course. Every time a friend welcomed a blessed bundle, I would visit for the compulsory coo and hold. But that was the extent of my experience. I wasn't so sure I would know what to do when it came to my own.

I remember casually expressing concerns at my baby shower. The aunts and cousins—already veterans in the art of raising kids—assured me that once my baby arrived, I would know what to do. I would know what his cries meant. "It will come to you. You'll see," they said, making this motherly intuition sound like a car battery just waiting to be sparked by jumper cables. My oldest is eleven. I'm still waiting for this magical instinct to kick in. What we hear is that maternal instinct will help us master the basics, like discerning the hungry cry from the wet diaper cry, soothing a child to sleep, and knowing when to potty train.

And of course there is nothing more natural than breastfeeding, right? "Just put him on your chest, and you both will figure it out," moms are told. "It's what your breasts were meant for." What happens when it's all so damn hard? Why are some of us so innately nurturing and others have to diligently work at what should be a natural state of being? Could science really explain this natural ability to nurture, to have the innate ability to be like every TV mom we grew up idolizing?

If you think about it, our DNA can tell us a lot about ourselves. The most basic characteristics are formed even before we emerge from the birth canal. Have a pair of Y chromosomes and a boy is on the way. End up with X's, and you've got yourself a girl. Whether you are a night owl or an early riser is associated with the PER3 sequence. Have a particular variation of the FTO gene and you are more likely to end up obese. If you are lucky enough to have the klotho gene, you will live a long life, and thrill seekers have a gene that is associated with impulsiveness. What if a gene could also predict our ability to nurture? What if a gene could predict how we react to early motherhood?

It's a question science has tried to answer since the early 1990s when Harvard Medical School doctoral student Jennifer Brown noticed something was very wrong with the entire litter of mice pups she was observing. They were dying a day after being born. It was odd because the pups were healthy, as was their mom. The problem was that the mom had no interest in caring for or feeding them. Instead, the pups were left to starve. You see, the mothers were purposely bred without a gene called fosB and that created a nurturing defect. Turns out, this gene is a critical component in regulating hormones related to maternal behavior and usually just being around your baby will trigger it.[1]

Though the news went largely unnoticed, this was the world's first hint that there may actually be a real mom gene.

Many years later, another group of researchers found that the Peg1/Mest and Peg3 genes also negatively affect motherly tendencies in mice when disabled by scientists.[2] The issue resurfaced yet again in 2012 when researchers at Rockefeller University studied female mice with babies for clues as to what activates the maternal instinct. They believe there is a single gene that could be responsible for motivating mothers to protect, feed, and raise their offspring. And since mice and humans share many of the same genes, there is a good argument that these genes also influence our maternal instincts. But was this enough to really explain why some of us don't feel as though we have an innate maternal vibe?

A Complicated Beginning

I had to admit to myself that as fascinating as the research is, maternal (and paternal) instinct in humans is far more nuanced than biology alone. In earlier chapters, I delved into expectations our society places on mothers, which is only rivaled by the pressure we put on ourselves. How we feel about our abilities as a mother can be heavily influenced by many factors, including our birth stories.

My own entry into motherhood was punctuated by fear and anxiety. My pregnancy was wrought with medical complications. I had gestational diabetes and preeclampsia. I was even hospitalized at twenty-four weeks when my blood pressure rose to a dangerously high level and they discussed delivering the baby that day. Things were up and down throughout, and I ended up having an emergency cesarean section at thirty-four and a half weeks.

After Lex was born, he wasn't placed on my chest like I had expected. No teary, bonding moment for us. Instead, he was rushed to the NICU. My doctor did not place me on the maternity ward, so I wouldn't be saddened by the cries from babies in rooms with their mothers. It was such a thoughtful gesture and one I am grateful for to this day.

Lex was delivered before developing the suck-swallow-breathe reflex in utero, so he couldn't breastfeed just yet. Instead, I pumped all day, every day, and he was fed through little tubes in his nose. To say this was hard is a gross understatement. After five days, I was discharged without my baby. For weeks, I sat next to his bassinet in the NICU all day, willing him to eat from a bottle.

As time passed, I inevitably got to know other babies, and there were rows and rows of babies too ill or under-developed to go home. Only a few moms were there every day like I was. I was stunned by the lack of visitors. Some of the babies had been there so long that parents had to go back to work or tend to other children.

It was hard not to bond with the one other mom always there hovering like I was. There was a kinship, linked by our shared anguish. Her son's oxygen levels would drop without warning, causing the alarms to blare at random times. We traded magazines, talked about our jobs, which nurses we liked most, which we liked least, and what it would be like to have our babies home. "Whatever you do, don't ever let them put your baby in room 211," she whispered when we pass a big yellow door as we returned from a short retreat to the cafeteria for a snack. "That room is for the really sick babies. Those babies are never leaving."

It was noted: pray your baby never sees the inside of room 211. The weeks wore on, and I got to know the stories of the various babies thanks to chatty staff. Ben's mom was never here because she had five other kids at home. Sarah's parents' marriage could not take the strain of her hospitalization and were already headed for divorce. It was a surreal way to start new motherhood, but the only one I knew at that point. When I got the green light to take Lex home on day thirty, I was elated until the nurse said that for his last night, he would be transferred to room 211 because they needed his NICU incubator for a newer newborn. I freaked out. I immediately started crying, refusing to have him moved. They assured me that all was fine and he would be leaving in the morning.

He did move to 211, and he did go home in the morning. But there was something so scarring about the entire experience. Everything about motherhood up to that point had been terrifying. It was hard not to feel that I had failed in some way by not giving him a smoother entry into the world.

I'm Not Supposed to Feel This Way

Most transitions into motherhood are far less dramatic, thank goodness. Still, many women shared how unsettled they were in those first weeks, months, even years. "All of the sudden you think you're an animal if you're just not feeling it," said mother-of-three Deborah, an intuitive life coach. "We're supposed to love, and I don't know a mother out there who doesn't adore their kids. It's not about their kids; it's about the role of motherhood. So I always say I love my kids, but I don't love motherhood."

That's an admission that most moms are unwilling to voice. There is a high amount of shame associated with not loving motherhood or feeling as though you are failing at something that seems to come so easily to others. "I felt like he just didn't want to be a part of our family," Meghan said of her second baby. "He cried all the time. I couldn't get him to calm down."

Not surprisingly, breastfeeding is another emotional touchstone. In the moments leading up to every feeding of Aidan, my second child, I swear I heard the theme music from *Psycho*, knowing that my poor nipple would be gnawed to within an inch of its existence. It's supposed to be the most "natural" thing a woman can do, but research suggests many women struggle with it. According to a study that included 1,011 mother-newborn pairs, about 85 percent of pregnant women intend to breastfeed for at least three months, but only one-third actually make it that long.[3] New moms quit for several reasons, including worrying the baby is not getting enough to eat, going back to work, and difficulty even getting the baby to latch. It's hard not to think, *I'm a failure. I'm terrible at this.*

Part of the problem is that women feel they cannot express how unexpectedly distressing the experience is without looking like a bad mom. It's a dilemma many relate to. Becoming a mother made me feel like I was a passenger on that carnival ride that spins so fast the gravitational force keeps you stuck to the wall. I was scared and uncertain how I would feel from one moment to the next. And there was an all-consuming anxiety that I was never doing anything well—not mothering, not marriage, and certainly not work.

Men also buy into the notion that new mothers should be filled with nothing but joy. Whenever I was honest about my feelings to someone who asked how I was doing as a new mom, my husband fretted. "It makes you sound so ungrateful." I felt instant shame, like a kid being scolded for stealing candy from a convenience store. But it's not like I expected to feel this way. No woman does.

"Am I a good mother?" is the prevailing question, sometimes uttered out loud but more often only as a silent torment. They weren't prepared for how much work it all actually is and often felt more frustration than bliss. It wasn't supposed to be this way, they lamented. What became apparent after so many interviews is that these doubts and fears are a natural part of parenthood. Not for all women, of course, but for most.

Our own childhoods are a huge factor in how we adjust to motherhood as well. How were you raised? What were your parents like? What kind of feelings did they express about the pressures of parenting? Were you encouraged to be maternal? Did you have a very affectionate family? Did you help raise younger siblings?

Your adult lifestyle also plays a part. Having a partner, job security, and a good support system can make becoming a parent all the more desirous. Though nothing guarantees parenting will come easy for any of us. Perhaps the most important lesson you can take away from this book is that **love is innate; parenting skills are not**. They are learned. You will see other mothers who seem more patient, more doting, more together. You imagined that you would never yell or look a hot mess or ever feel an inkling of resentment, yet you do. And that is okay. That is normal.

We have a tendency to misinterpret not enjoying motherhood with the fear that we are not cut out for it. There is a danger in that. There is a tremendous amount of shame when we have frustration, anger, anxiety, or even depression as parents. "I don't want a parent to feel guilty when they have the normal range of human emotion," stressed McCaslin. "And those are normal emotions. We have enough guilt as it is."

The Big Lie

Here is the truth of the matter: The whole idea of a maternal instinct sets us up to feel like failures. It makes us feel like unworthy outliers in a world of perfect mothers. What's especially maddening is that there is an expectation of this maternal behavior long before we are even mothers. So how do you survive this stage?

It starts with changing your expectations of yourself and the experience. Deborah's sister gave her perhaps the best advice I've ever heard. "She said don't think you're going to feel this immense love right away because you might not," she recounted gratefully. "And if you don't, you might not because your delivery might be hard, you'll be exhausted, and so if you don't feel good in that moment that has nothing to do with your love for your baby. I remember taking that in, really listening, and thinking, *Okay, I'm going to lessen all my expectations of the moment of birth*. Because we all know when we have high expectations, they're never met." In actuality, that should be our mindset throughout every stage of parenthood.

The disconnect between what we expect and what we experience can even affect our emotional health. During this time, the question you need to hear most is, "How are *you* doing?" Just think about the shocked and teary response Meghan Markle had after being asked that simple question after the birth of her son Archie. "Not many people have asked if I'm okay . . . it's a very real thing to be going through behind the scenes," she told the interviewer.[4] Alternating bouts of cheerfulness and sadness are normal, but not enough women are prepared for the minefield of emotions that often comes with new motherhood.

"With my clients, I often describe it like this: Have you ever worked all day in a room and it starts to get dark and you don't even notice it's dark out?" detailed Dr. Athan, who teaches a class on perinatal mental health at Columbia University. "You've been working in the dark, and your partner or friend comes in and asks, 'Do you want to turn a light on?' You didn't realize it because it just happened gradually over time. That can be the experience of depression a lot of times, where you don't even see it yourself. It takes someone else to say you really don't seem like yourself. Things aren't always so acutely obvious. And depression can narrow your cognitive visual field." Essentially, you may not even realize something is wrong.

It's important to know the difference between mommy burnout and baby blues and something more sinister. And every new mother, whether you gave birth, adopted, or used a surrogate, can experience postpartum depression, warned Mullin: "It can be an overwhelming experience for everyone." Even when you look at the

DSM-5, which is the *Diagnostic and Statistical Manual of Mental Disorders*, it can be confusing.

You don't have to be a hypochondriac to wonder if you have an illness as you scan through the common symptoms. The determining factor is degree and frequency. How often are you feeling down? How long does it go on for? How difficult is it to recover and the refractory period to return? Do you have a history of it? There is no shame in this. We all need a little extra help to get better some times.

PMAD Primer

Perinatal and postpartum mood and anxiety disorder (PMAD) is a catchall term for all the distressing feelings that may come up during pregnancy and after you give birth. Like most mental health conditions, PMADs are caused by a combination of biological, psychological, and social factors. After we give birth, our estrogen and progesterone take a deep dive, which can affect mood and emotional state. A woman is further at risk if she has a family history of mental illness. Another factor is when a woman feels that she is lacking support for this new, often daunting phase of life.

BABY BLUES. Having a baby is a huge adjustment. Between 60 and 80 percent of new moms will experience the baby blues, which is indicated by feelings of sadness, frustration, and irritability.[5] Often confused with postpartum depression, it begins anywhere from one to three days after delivery but only lasts up to two weeks. It typically resolves on its own.

POSTPARTUM DEPRESSION. At least 15 percent of new mothers will experience postpartum depression in the twelve months after giving birth, confirm mental health experts.[6] Moms believe that number may be even higher considering that a lot of women don't seek help. Postpartum depression is marked by sadness, crying, anxiety, low energy, changes in appetite and sleep, and feelings of guilt and shame. Some women even report thoughts of harming themselves or their baby. Share what you are experiencing during your six-week checkup so you and your doctor can determine if treatment is needed. Reach out for help sooner if you're at all concerned.

POSTPARTUM ANXIETY. Affecting one in every ten women, postpartum anxiety can cause constant worry, fear something bad will happen, trouble sleeping, dizziness, and heart palpitations.[7] In the more extreme cases, these symptoms affect your ability to function throughout the day, and medical intervention may be necessary.

POSTPARTUM OBSESSIVE-COMPULSIVE DISORDER (OCD). Women who suffer from obsessive, repetitive thoughts about their baby or compulsions to constantly clean or check things may have postpartum OCD. It afflicts between 3 to 5 percent of new mothers. This may get worse without treatment.[8]

POSTPARTUM PSYCHOSIS. Are you seeing and hearing things other people are not? Feeling as though people are out to get you, or having strange thoughts about your child? If so, you could be suffering from postpartum psychosis.

It is very rare, only afflicting 0.2 percent of all new mothers, but requires immediate medical help.[9]

If you worry you have a PMAD, the best thing you can do is talk to a mental health professional. However, if you suspect a friend is suffering but is reluctant to get help, continue to support her without pressing too hard. Cook her meals, visit, offer to watch the baby, tell her partner or a family member what you believe is going on. "When working with patients who are not yet ready to make important changes, psychologists and therapists use a technique called rolling with resistance," explained Dr. Emily Guarnotta, a clinical psychologist in Long Island, New York, who specializes in perinatal mood and anxiety disorders.

"It involves acknowledging that the person is ambivalent about change, in this case getting treatment for a PMAD. You simply listen, gently suggest how treatment might help, and avoid pushing the person toward change. You can also ask your friend what is stopping her from getting help. Maybe she feels that she doesn't have time, feels ashamed, or doesn't know where to start. This will give you an idea of how you can help. For example, you can offer to help her find a therapist or try to reduce the stigma of getting help for a PMAD."

Love Is Stronger Than Instinct

The bottom line is that maternal instinct is tantamount to cultural lore. You don't have to be a baby person to be a good mother. You don't have to know what that cry means to give wonderful care. We are so accustomed to evaluating and comparing ourselves to other mothers. This is a surefire recipe for feeling like a failure.

Actually, the fact that you are even worried about being maternal is a sign of how much you care about your child. Are your kids happy? Are your kids loved? Are your kids cared for? Do you protect them? You are developing a relationship with your child. The more you get to know them, the more comfortable you will feel as a parent. Are there things you could improve upon? That is true for every human being whether you are a parent or not. Your kids don't need another kind of mom. You are enough.

YOUR NEW TO-DO LIST

WHAT YOU DON'T HAVE TO DO

Always want to be around your child.

Love parenting all the time.

Put your needs last.

Be happy staying at home with the kids all day.

Handle the kids without needing a break.

Never be resentful of how difficult motherhood can be.

Never reminisce about life before kids.

WHAT YOU NEED TO DO

Accept that loving your child
is what matters most.

How you feel matters. Talk to someone
about what you are going through.

Love what makes you a unique mom.

Don't take your child's misbehavior personally.

Stop wishing you were like that perfect
mom on Instagram. It's fake. Everyone's
toddlers are total nightmares.

Don't be ashamed of your mistakes.
Everyone makes them.

Be patient with yourself. You don't get one
chance to do it right. Parenting is a learning
process for all of us. As a result, we become
better moms with each passing day.

Nine

The Single-Minded

WHAT TO REALLY EXPECT:
Some people will make unfair assumptions
about your life. Some people are just idiots.
You know who you are, they don't.

One morning, I sat listening to a group of moms catch up over coffee. It had become a ritual among this cohort, mingling for a bit before rushing off to the office (for those that worked) or back home to manage whatever the day required. The banter was lively, filled with plenty of inside jokes, gossip, and inevitably, complaints about partners. One woman, whose husband travels several days a week, bemoaned how hard it is to juggle everything solo most of the time. "You are basically a single mom," one friend sympathetically offered. The others nodded in agreement. I turned my attention to the only actual single mom in the group. She didn't seem bothered by the equivocation.

Motherhood can be hard on us all no matter the relationship status, but let's get real here. What single parents go through is not the same, not by a long shot. Among the fears they shared with me are carrying the financial load alone, wondering how this will affect their child, being a stereotype, feeling overwhelmed, being enough. It's all so dizzying and not just because of all that is on their plate. There are a different set of unspoken rules for them, subtle and sometimes not-so-subtle nuances of parenting life that are specific to the single mom.

How Did We Get Here?

We should ask ourselves what it really means to be a progressive society. Is it measured by technological advances? The strength of the economy? Or is it how accepting we are of difference, especially when it comes to people's personal lives? We have certainly made many strides in some areas (though long overdue, gay couples finally have the right to marry). Why then is the image of a man, a woman, and two and half children still considered the perfect family structure?

It makes no sense when you consider what families in America really look like these days. There are 21.9 million children being raised by a single parent in the United States.[1] To put it in perspective, that is more than one-quarter of all children under age twenty-one in this country. A majority of single-parent homes are headed up by a mom, nearly three million children are raised by grandparents, and 24 percent of young women say they don't plan to have children and 34 percent are not sure they ever will.[2] Is a childless couple any less of a family?

Even if we don't fit the perfect family mold, we often wish we did. It can be a crippling thought when you become a single parent whether it's by chance or by choice.

"I had a lot of mom guilt because of this," admitted Kasi, an Atlanta mom raising her son solo. "I wanted to do the kid thing the right way. I didn't want to have a kid out of wedlock. I wanted to at least do it with a partner. In love, together, an idealistic relationship." These feelings persist even though she is a professional with her own accounting business and has created a supportive network of family and friends to surround her son. "I feel bad that my son doesn't have a dad that is present," she worried. "I feel like I failed him in that way because he should have that." It's a disquieting feeling that's hard to shake.

Adding to that anxiety is the pecking order that exists in the world of single parents. My conversation with mothers has shown me that how one becomes a single mom has a tremendous impact on both how she feels about herself and how others perceive her. Widows are at the top of the pyramid. It's an unimaginable circumstance for a parent of young children, to be sure. And that status guarantees both reverence and respect.

Next would be those who divorce and are afforded a certain level of respect because, though they are single now, they started their families "the right way." Now it's a completely different story for women who are single moms from the start. This group often feels blamed for what people like to call their "bad choices."

Just remember, you don't have to explain your life to anyone. My hope is that this chapter prepares you for those misconceptions and helps you combat any feelings of insecurity, fear, and doubt.

Breaking Up a Happy Home

More than the typical mommy guilt about whether you are spending enough quality time with your kids, single moms also carry a unique emotional burden. "Now they have two homes," said Deborah, who divorced her spouse when her boys were in grade school. "You feel guilty because you're uprooting them; you're putting your own needs first." For those who are wrestling with this, remember that keeping your child in an unhappy environment just to keep the family together may have a detrimental effect.

To choose emotional stability and happiness can be an invaluable example to set for your children, promised Deborah: "I would have been miserable had I stayed, and I definitely give them a much better life being true to myself, than not being true to myself. And I do tell them that too. This part of my life doesn't make me happy; this part does. I try to show them, 'You're going to have that in your life too.'" One of the greatest fears single moms shared was that their children will somehow suffer, that they won't be as happy or as successful or as prepared for the world.

A 2017 study by the European Society of Human Reproduction and Embryology compared the well-being of children of single mothers and those from two-parent families. Guess what? They found no difference in the success of the parent-child relationship or how the children develop. However, the findings indicated one very significant difference: single mothers by choice tended to have a supportive social network.[3]

Solo Act

One of the most emotionally taxing aspects of single motherhood is dealing with an ex. Remember, you are single but not alone. According to Pew Research, by the age of nine, one in five children will experience a parent breakup.[4] And if you are co-parenting with an ex, often everything becomes a negotiation. How to discipline, who gets what holiday, where to send the kids to school, and the list goes on.

Look at this as a part of your ongoing evolution as a mom. It will require patience, understanding, and the ability to let go of some irksome behavior, but you can do this. To successfully co-parent, it's all about being collaborative for the sake of your child. I know that is easier said than done. These tips will help:

1. Work on healing your wounds from the relationship. Consider seeing a therapist to talk about what you've been through and get guidance on how to move forward in a positive, emotionally healthy way.

2. If interactions with your ex are particularly difficult, consider making it more of a businesslike relationship where the parameters are clearly written out. That way there is no confusion or arguments over something not being clear.

3. Don't argue in front of your kids. In the same vein, don't bad-mouth your ex in front of them either. However, having a calm discussion in front of them can provide a wonderful example of how you can work things out amicably.

4. If you can tolerate spending time with your ex, consider sharing major holidays or birthdays. Even when parents are divorced, kids can benefit from united family time. One particularly saintly mom shared how she even welcomed the mistress-turned-new-wife into the fold, inviting her over for Thanksgiving and other family events. "I did it for my kids," she said. "I want them to have a good relationship with their father and *her*. She is their stepmom now."

On the other end of the spectrum are the mothers who are shouldering the burden all by themselves. Who will I share the responsibility with if something goes wrong? How will I pay for school? How do I manage pickup, drop-off, and sick days alongside a full-time job?

The juggle is real. It's normal to worry but not to the point that it hinders you from moving forward. I marveled at what Tomika has been able to accomplish in the last five years. It wasn't easy, and there were setbacks, but she ventured into the unknown, working contractually while mapping out and then creating her ideal career. In addition to being an in-demand content creator, she founded the Motivated Mamas life coaching service designed for single moms and the Single Parents Who Travel Facebook group, which has more than seven thousand members worldwide. There will be setbacks and even stalls, but pace yourself so as not to burn out.

Race

Race can add another level of complexity to the struggles of the single mom. "I'm a stereotype," said Tomika, who is raising her son solo after an unplanned pregnancy. "I'm a Black woman who's raising a Black child. Of course, you know, immediately the welfare trope, what that means historically, and the racism that brings all that about. What flashed through my head was the story a mentor told me. She's a world-class author, journalist, and activist. She talked about how she wore a ring to her doctors' appointments every time she went in to get a checkup on her baby because she felt like she was going to be judged. And so I had to do some coaching of myself, around not allowing myself to make this joyous experience into something negative and to remind myself that I know who I am and I am nobody else's perception of me."

The Scarlet Letter

Those perceptions, however, can make for awkward encounters. Several single moms talked of being labeled a spouse stealer. One divorcee recalled how other moms would eye her suspiciously if she spoke too closely with husbands or wore something a little clingy. "I'm single because my husband was cheating on me," she shared in tone marked by bitterness and incredulity. "Why would I want someone else's slime-ball husband? It's ridiculous."

If this happens to you, try to remember that any side-eye has more to do with how they feel about themselves and their relationship than about you. It's easier to simply pity them than try to convince them otherwise.

Another complaint: being excluded from social events. Single moms also experienced not being invited to certain playdates, dinners, or gatherings because of their relationship status.

The excuse is often something along the lines of, "I didn't want you to feel uncomfortable in a group full of couples." In a situation like this, consider explaining why this assumption is unfair and even hurtful. What should follow is an apology for making you feel like an outcast because of your relationship status. If she's not contrite, perhaps this isn't the type of friend you want to spend your precious free time with anyway.

There can also be frustrations with child-free friends. "They don't get it because they automatically stop inviting you or including you, and you feel so ostracized," confessed one mother. "Even if you can't make it, because you can't, generally—or you don't want to—you still want to be included. You kind of just have to start watching everything happen on social media that you didn't even know was happening. They stop thinking about you as an inclusive part of their crew because you're a parent now. It made going into motherhood the loneliest time ever. I was really depressed."

The Support You Need

Some moms shared a reluctance to ask for help because they think it suggests that they are failing. You may not realize this, but it's likely you do have a co-parent, just not one that was once an intimate partner. A co-parent is not limited to those we once had a romantic relationship with. "Unmarried women who don't have intimate partners are going through this transition with their parents, the grandparents, or a close friend," advised Dr. Phil Cowan. "There are almost always at least two people who are parenting this child, and how they are doing as individuals and how they are doing in a relationship with Mom makes a difference."

That means you have to assess that relationship in the same way married moms do with their spouses: Is there a history of anxiety and depression? How competent and confident is this co-parent? How do they handle conflict and disagreements? One thing that is difficult for single moms is to admonish or disagree with their own parents, but it's important to establish rules and boundaries.

Oftentimes, the way we see our parents changes after we have our own children. We realized that our parents, like we are now, were just people trying to figure out the best way. It humanizes them like no other shared experience. We feel more compassion and less judgment. So if you think you are parenting alone, you are deluding yourself.

It's also critically important to surround yourself with other single moms who don't let their status psychologically cripple them. A friend who is continually pessimistic about being a single mom can be more emotionally damaging than you realize. The people in your support network should lift you up, not bring you down. You will face enough negativity from the outside world; you don't need to deal with it from a confidante. How relationships make you feel is very important —all our relationships. That includes intimate ones.

To Date or Not to Date

I talked to many single moms who say that dating is just not a priority. Understandably, it's hard to wrap your mind around investing time and energy into yet another relationship. Sometimes you will worry about bringing "complications" into a new romance. "When you're trying to start dating and you have a young baby, and you're explaining that to a guy—it's like you want to leave it out," confessed Kasi, who was never in a committed relationship with the father of her son. "But you can't leave it out! Now when I meet a guy, I have to say, 'Yeah, I'm a great girl, you know, I have this going on, that going on—oh, but I do have a young son.' And it's almost like you feel apologetic for it. There are certain guys I won't even go for because I feel that it's out of my league now. He's not going to want to deal with this."

Fear of rejection is normal, but companionship is key. If it is something you crave, it is something you deserve. There are certain things you should look out for. Not everyone is a good fit for your family, and this person needs to be a match for your child too.

DATING MATERIAL CHECKLIST

- They like children and embrace the fact that I have them.

- They understand that I need to spend most of my time with my child.

- They want to be involved with my family and plan activities together.

- They respect the boundaries that I have in place for how they communicate with my child.

- They understand if I need to cancel last minute because of an incident with explosive diarrhea or some other common parenting disaster.

- They have goals and plans for their own lives that are flexible enough to include my family.

You do the work of two parents and often without the emotional support you want. More than any of us, those pulling double duty need to work hard at not losing themselves in the tsunami of job and family life. People will wonder how you do it. Hell, sometimes you will wonder how you do it, but you do. You are going to feel exhausted at times, maybe even most of the time. There are so many unknowns right now, and it will cause some sleepless nights. It's important to remember that you don't need to prove anything to anyone but yourself.

YOUR NEW TO-DO LIST

1. Establish boundaries with the important people in your life. Let them know what you expect and in return listen to what they expect and need from you.

2. Take advantage of the help offered. Being a single mom doesn't mean you have to go it alone all the time. Ask friends and relatives to babysit so you can take time for yourself. Some moms set up a weekly babysitting

duty swap with other single parents so
they have alone time they can count on.

3. Create a vision board of goals and dreams you
   have for yourself and your child. Then create
   a ten-step plan for accomplishing them.

4. Create a community of people who understand
   and support you. This can be other single parents
   or just wonderful people you can open up to.

Ten

It's Mommy's Turn to Wine

WHAT TO REALLY EXPECT:
Our mommy juice culture
is as dangerous as it is fun.

My kindergartner filled out a 'My Mother' Q&A sheet that they do every year for Mother's Day and ID'd my favorite food as 'wine.' AGAIN. Oy!" a friend wrote in a recent Facebook post. *Hilarious*, I thought. We all know the running joke about moms and booze in our culture. The word is, kids will drive you to drink. A lot. We've seen entire movies dedicated to it and reality shows that make it appear as essential as breathing (just check out the *Real Housewives* of any city). Then there is the endless parade of memes to remind us:

Motherhood. Powered by love. Fueled
by coffee. Sustained by wine.

The most expensive part of having kids
is all the wine you need to drink.

Mom status: Currently holding it
all together with alcohol.

No surprise winemakers are capitalizing on the trend, targeting stressed-out moms specifically with not-so-subtle brands like Mommy's Time Out and Mad Housewife Cellars. It's a trope we readily buy into because, hell, it's fun. It grants us permission to be something other than the diaper changers, playdate schedulers, laundry washers, and dinner makers we might feel we have morphed into. Many moms, myself included, enjoyed social drinking before becoming parents, and afterward we enjoy it even more.

One of the biggest ironies of motherhood is that it both expands and contracts your world at the same time. You have this new person in your life, but the rest of your world may feel as though it gets smaller. You are not interacting or involved the same way. There is a loss of self. A loss of independence. At the same time, you love your baby beyond measure. It's a weird tension. Enjoying a drink is a small way we can reclaim a part of that other, longed-for life. It's taking back a little piece of that independence.

If our lives were to play out on the big screen, our kids would undoubtedly take on the role of the chaos-inducing crime lords, and a nice bottle of red would surely be the bustier-clad heroine bringing us back from the brink of madness. It's not about hating motherhood or just drowning our sorrows. This—we have been instructed by pop culture—is how moms relax and have fun.

My apartment building in New York City happened to have a slew of new moms, all of us desperate to commiserate after work each day. In the evenings, we would relieve our sitters, get the children in their jammies, and meet up at one of our places. Alcohol was as much a play-date staple as Play-Doh. Vodka-lemonade was the drink du jour at a mom's place on the second floor. Cabernet was plentiful in 9B. Unit 3F always had a nice white chilling in the fridge.

The kids would run around, their playful screams drowned out by our own bonding between sips of whatever. We moms were all scrambling to keep it all together—work, home, kids, marriage. This was our reward. This eased the tensions of the day. It was a brief respite from the pandemonium that seemed to swallow us whole.

Other moms echoed this sentiment across the country. A glass while preparing dinner, a generous pour after finally getting the kids to sleep. As tough as the infancy stage is, it gets even more exhausting as they start to crawl, pop choking hazards in their mouths, and learn to climb out of their cribs. I remember meeting a woman at the park one Saturday afternoon, both of us with large, disposable coffee cups in hand. Mine held a triple espresso. Hers, however, was filled with a full-bodied red. Ingenious, I marveled.

We saw nothing strange in this. But for a growing population of moms, a harmless, fun indulgence slowly morphs into addiction. In the last five years, clinicians across the country say there has been a sharp rise in the number of moms seeking treatment for alcoholism.

Research from the National Institute on Alcohol Abuse and Alcoholism (NIAAA) shows that alcohol use disorder in US women doubled from 2002 to 2013.[1] During the same time period, another study by the National

Epidemiologic Survey on Alcohol and Related Conditions found a 58 percent rise in the number of women who consume more than four drinks a day, a number indicative of a drinking problem.[2]

How Did We Get Here?

The "Mommy needs wine" messaging certainly feels like harmless fun, and the world tells us as much. It was, to each of us, a well-deserved coping mechanism for the pressures of parenthood. These binges have been normalized, and therein lies the problem. Mothers are told it's okay to deal with the stress and anxiety of parenthood with a drink, or two, or a whole bottle.

Laura McKowen, a prominent voice in addiction recovery who runs online sobriety support meetings through LauraMcKowen.com, warned about the almost imperceptible shift that happens for some. "Many of us drink before we have kids, but after, it has a different effect. That is something I hear a lot from the mothers I work with. Their drinking substantially changes. It becomes kind of a need for when you're getting a little edgy or your nerves are shot. And so that glass of wine becomes really important."

If you take nothing else away from this chapter, please remember this: a drink should be something you enjoy, not something you need to get through the moment, the task, the day.

A study conducted by Caron Treatment Centers, an in-patient program with facilities in Pennsylvania and Florida, found the top reasons mothers turn to alcohol are stress, anxiety, problems in romantic relationships, pressure from family or friends, traumatic experience, and boredom.[3] Nearly every woman I interviewed experienced a combination of these factors.

Admittedly, a certain degree of physical and emotional upheaval is par for the course with parenthood. The unusual part is the way our culture actually encourages us to drink in order to deal. I remember seeing a baby sporting a onesie that announced, "I'm the reason mommy drinks." It's supposed to be funny, cute, and relatable, but it's also deeply disturbing. Can you imagine if we encouraged any other stressed-out, overburdened, and exhausted group of people to soothe their fraught emotions with alcohol? That would be grossly irresponsible at best.

Today it's wine, but decades ago it was pills used to mollify frazzled moms. In the 1960s, doctors prescribed benzodiazepines, like Valium. Dubbed "mother's little helper," it quickly became the most prescribed drug in the world and even the subject of a Rolling Stones hit by the same name.[4]

By the 1980s, researchers warned that long-term use comes with serious risks, like memory loss, anxiety, and depression.[5] And wine, of course, was a far more suitable soother. For generations, women have been dealing with the same pressures: clean home, well-behaved children, happy spouses, and successful career.

Like so many, those pressures became too much for Amy, an Allentown, Pennsylvania, mom of one. "No one ever told me that I needed to have a master's degree and 2.5 kids to live happily ever after, but that is what I saw in my family and my community, and that's what I thought

I was supposed to be," she said. Amy did earn a degree and had one successful pregnancy, but three miscarriages and a failing relationship weighed heavily on her. The social drinking with friends and neighbors soon became something much more sinister.

"I didn't realize it at the time, but I was numbing myself with alcohol so I didn't have to deal, and my drinking went to the extreme real fast," she added. "I turned to alcohol as a coping skill." After two years, she couldn't hide her problem anymore, and her family encouraged her to seek help.

Lauren shared her own rock bottom, the moment she knew she had to stop drinking. On July 13, 2013, she got blackout drunk at her brother's wedding and left her four-year-old daughter alone in a hotel room the entire night. In truth, she says, it was one of many poor choices she made while drinking, but this one was different. As she describes in her beautiful and breathtakingly honest memoir, *We Are the Luckiest: The Surprising Magic of a Sober Life*:

> That night, the two worlds I'd been trying so diligently to keep separate collided: my interior life, full of secrets and coverups, nightly blackouts with wine and Ambien, crushing anxiety and exhaustion, and a growing fear of myself; and my external one, where I hosted dinner parties and bought my daughter to playdates, got better jobs and more promotions, dressed well, and regularly ran six miles around Boston at lunch.

This is the duality mothers who have a substance problem or fear that they do often describe. In many ways, they are enabled by a culture that still holds a very narrow view of what it means to be an alcoholic. I remember a parent setting tongues wagging at the annual holiday fair at my son's school after having too many mimosas from the bar station. She was fall-down drunk. A couple of moms had to help her out to a cab. From that point on, she was commonly referred to as Black Hawk Down (behind her back). Everyone assumed she had a "real" problem and talked of other alleged incidents.

In reality, it isn't always so obvious. "I was totally high-functioning until I wasn't," Amy shared with me. "I was a classroom mom; I was involved in the PTO stuff at school. I covered for myself really well. I made sure everything on the outside looked pretty when I was struggling on the inside. My son was four when this was going on. My priority was always him in the sense that his homework was done and he was at everything he needed to be. I was drinking all day long, but as it got later in the day and he was getting ready for bed, my drinking really escalated."

Keep in mind that having alcoholism or being an alcoholic isn't necessarily about how often someone is drinking. "It's really about what's happening once they start," explained Erin Goodhart, director of Women's Services at Caron Treatment. "If a mom went to a birthday party and swore she was only going to have one drink but then ended up drinking so much she embarrassed her kids—that's a red flag. Also, if you are craving it throughout the day, drinking out of anxiety or fear, or don't have any other way to relax, you are moving into a problematic state."

Most of us have encountered a friend whose drinking is a concern. This issue is a lot more common than we are comfortable talking about—though we should. Often it's fear of losing a friendship that keeps us from stepping in. That was my main concern when Allison suggested we sit down with our friend Connie to talk about her drinking.

I was horrified at the thought. I tried to come up with an excuse to avoid the entire plan. Does she really have a problem? We all drink, so does that make us hypocrites for saying something? What if she never speaks to me again? Allison insisted we needed to make sure everything "was okay with her." Was her drinking masking something she needed to talk about? Was she trying to excise some negative emotion with glass after glass of wine? We didn't think she was an alcoholic, per se; we just wanted to head off a burgeoning problem, if there was one. Still, I dreaded the idea of approaching her.

The morning of this so-called intervention, I sat in a coffee shop next to Allison, heart racing, blood pressure surely surging, dreading the conversation to come. When our friend arrived, we filled a half hour with trivial small talk about other dramas among our circle of friends. Did you hear that so-and-so wants a divorce? Do you think that dad is too flirty? What are you going to do for spring break? Then, the moment of truth arrived.

"Well, dear," Allison began, as she did most tough conversations. "We wanted to talk to you because we are concerned . . ." I cringed throughout. Connie's reaction: gratitude. Honest-to-God gratitude. She was so touched that we loved her enough to check in and make sure everything was okay. And it was.

The moment had a tremendous impact on me for two reasons: Our friend took it as a sign of how much we love her, and we do. And secondly, while this informal intervention felt clumsy and awkward, it was the right thing to do. Most of us are not experienced in these types of conversations, so I turned to Julie Maida, founder of the internet support space SoberMommies.com. Since so many people do not have the support they need, she stresses that the most critical way we can help someone struggling is by offering to simply be present for them.

HOW TO TALK TO A FRIEND ABOUT HER DRINKING

1. Reach out. "The love and trust of that relationship can help somebody in ways that we can't even imagine," instructed Maida. "Just by sitting next to somebody and saying I understand that you're struggling and I understand that you have no idea what you need right now, but I'm going to sit next to you, and either we can figure it out together, or we can not talk, and you can just know that I'm right here."

2. Express your concerns directly and suggest a change you can make together.

3. If she is making choices that put the kids in danger, share your concerns with her partner.

4. Suggest she seek help through therapy or a support group.

It's never easy to admit you have a problem. The humiliation of acknowledging such a thing keeps women quiet and tentative, preferring to ignore the painful truth. "There's nothing more shameful than being a mother who abuses alcohol in any way," McKowen shared. "In our society, there is a special place in hell for people like that. Not being able to 'handle' alcohol says something about your character, your self-control, and your ethics. So we work extra hard to keep it quiet." She knew that if she kept drinking, she would eventually lose custody of her daughter.

Sober since 2015, she credits Alcoholics Anonymous with saving her life, but writing, talking, and podcasting about her experience gave her newfound purpose and gave thousands of other struggling mothers hope. There was a voice they could connect to. The silence had been broken.

In addition to the overwhelming sense of shame, most women believe living a sober life or even just curbing the amount that they drink is tantamount to social suicide. "They don't know what their relationships will look like," she said. "They don't know how they'll ever have fun. They don't know who will hang out with them." There were plenty other worries associated with seeking sobriety.

BIGGEST FEARS OF SOBRIETY

1. "I'm not even sure I have an issue with alcohol." Just because you do not identify as an alcoholic doesn't mean you don't have a problem. Are you spending much of your time thinking about what you are drinking next, when you will be drinking, or whom

you will be drinking with? Are you spending too much time wondering how you are going to cover up your drinking? A yes answer to any of these questions is a red flag.

2. "I'm overwhelmed by the shame and stigma." In a culture where women feel the need to hide the fact they are formula-feeding their babies, it's no wonder they will not admit to an addiction. In reality, the people around us are witness to a lot of the things you do when drinking and are likely aware your drinking has become problematic. "Sometimes we are the last people to realize that everybody already knows," said Maida. "When we finally tell them we are cutting down or getting help, they are relieved and encouraging."

3. "Who will take care of my family while I'm in treatment?" Historically, women have always been the ones to provide the household support, make sure kids get to school, lunches are packed, explained Goodhart. "Time in treatment takes away time from their kids. Women feel shame even asking for help." But if you have a partner, this is the time for them to step up or to ask family and friends to help while you get better. Many treatment centers also offer virtual meetings for those who cannot leave for in-patient programs.

4. "There is alcohol everywhere I go." A lot of moms choose to avoid situations where there is temptation but that isn't always realistic. "If you feel obligated to go to a party or function where there is alcohol, you can go late and leave early," advised Amy, who has been

sober since 2015 and is now a substance abuse counselor. "You are there, you are seen. Do what you need to do and get out. Have an exit plan." Always take your car so if it gets uncomfortable or too much, you can just leave. If you are not open about your sobriety goals, take someone along who knows that the event may become uncomfortable for you and you will have support while you are there. Someone you can walk up to and say, "I need to go."

5. "I won't fit in with friends anymore." For many of us, quality time with mom friends means sharing a bottle or two. Your outings should not always only revolve around booze. If they do, suggest other activities you can do together. If they are not supportive of your choice to be sober, find new friends. Recovery can feel crippling and lonely without a supportive and encouraging group. McKowen and Maida have both made it their mission to link up women online and in person. "I cared so much about what people thought of me, what image I was portraying. Through recovery and working on myself, I let that all go," Amy confided. "There were definitely people in my community who look at me differently and judge me. Since I got sober, one close friend made it clear that she didn't like what I put my family through. I distanced myself. Our sons are still friends, but I engage with her as little as possible. In order for me to stay sober, I need supportive, positive people around me."

Acknowledging something needs to change is the first huge step. It's just as critical to find a resource to help you do that. And while AA and complete abstinence was the prevailing treatment for decades, experts now say there is no one-size-fits-all path to sobriety. Maida initially found recovery through a twelve-step program, but it required physical attendance at meetings for support. "When I had my youngest, I had a bout of postpartum depression that made it impossible for me to leave the house," she recalled. "I was so filled with anxiety that it was really difficult for me to go out. I thought going to a meeting can't possibly be the solution when I can't do it."

She was isolated and lonely and blamed her struggle on the fact she couldn't attend a meeting. Desperate to connect with others, she began writing about her life online.

Over a year's time, she found a sisterhood among other moms blogging about the ups and downs of motherhood. Then one day, she shared that she was sober. "The response I got was absolutely incredible," said Maida. "So many women said, 'I'm in recovery too, but I don't talk about it on my blog because I'm afraid of the stigma.' They were afraid people wouldn't read what they had to say and would judge their parenting if they knew." That set the seeds for her judgment-free Sober Mommies community for mothers figuring out their own sobriety journey. Women can anonymously share the realities of motherhood and recovery and, if they want, meet others on a similar journey.

"I wanted there to be a place that was no BS, no fluff," Maida said of the site that offers weekly support groups and various other resources. "There are posts all about how things improved and relationships that reconnected with sobriety, but there's also the posts on how much recovery sucks today or I am really angry I have to be sober when all my old friends are still drinking."

Having this type of recovery support is especially critical when the world experiences a disaster like the coronavirus pandemic. Not being able to go to a meeting because of the mandatory social isolation can create a lot of panic and uncertainty for someone working on their sobriety. What women like Maida and McKowen have created are spaces that do not require your physical presence to get the help that you need. It's a setup that works particularly well for mothers trying to balance home life, work, and sobriety.

This format allows for an even larger, more varied community of moms to seek help. Just as important, these sites are not just for people who identify as alcoholic. They are also resources for people who want a healthier relationship with alcohol. "Maybe they feel like they're drinking too much and they'd like to stop drinking as much but not completely," Maida offered. "There needs to be a place for those women. There needs to be a place to get support outside of abstinence or bust. I just think everybody deserves a safe place to feel encouraged regardless of their personal recovery choices."

Repairing What Is Broken

Until you get to the root of the issue, you will continue to find ways to numb out. And if you are wondering what life will be like on the other end of that tough sobriety journey, McKowen summed it up best: "Well, nothing is what I expected. Yes, I'm more aware. Definitely. I just feel like I'm actually in my life. I mean I'm here for it all. Whereas, I was just missing it all before and not even just because I was drinking, but because everything was in chaos. I was busy. I was checked out. So there's that. And that doesn't always feel good. That's not always like, *Yay, I'm aware*," she added laughing. "That actually is very difficult, but that's sort of what it means to be alive. I'm here for it all. I have self-respect; I have integrity. I never had that before. And there's this—like a real sense of peace and space in my life that I'd never expected to feel so wonderful."

The point of this chapter isn't to scare you or make you think you have a problem. Most women will never need to question their relationship with alcohol. But there can be a fine line between casual social drinking and numbing away angst with booze. Know the risks and more importantly, know how to help yourself and others.

YOUR NEW TO-DO LIST

1. **Consider going dry for one month.** If you can't, it's time to take a closer look at your relationship with alcohol.

2. **Have realistic expectations about what you can do.** It's okay to say no. It's important to avoid getting overwhelmed.

3. **Talk about the pressures you are experiencing.** It's easy for moms to feel bad about things, especially when it comes to their kids. It's important to express how you feel.

4. **Reexamine your relationships under a sober lens.** If your interactions with a friend or group of friends always involve alcohol, the connection may not be as authentic or deep as you think. You are each presenting an altered version of yourselves, and when you remove that, it becomes clear what the bond is based on. Do you still enjoy your time with them when sober? Do you have anything in common? Are you uplifted by your interactions?

5. **Authentic, genuine friends you can be honest with are a must.** Venting is very therapeutic, and if one mom is struggling with something, guaranteed at least three other moms are dealing with it too. One of the best things you can say to somebody who is struggling is "me too."

6. **Take care of your body.** Whether that means yoga, running, or another exercise, seek out a healthy release.

7. **Organize your world.** A messy environment often reflects how you feel on the inside.

8. **Have a positive relationship with yourself.** Get back to the things you love and you will be more content and less likely to need a substance to fill a void.

9. **Forgive yourself.** We moms exercise a lot of self-judgment, even self-hatred, in our daily lives. We pick apart our bodies, our parenting skills, and our ability to balance it all. Your first attempt at a sober life may not go as expected, but don't let this be another thing you beat yourself up about. Give yourself some much-needed grace.

Health Risks

Drinking in excess is bad for everyone, but there are particular health factors women should be aware of. We have less body water than men and, as such, can't tolerate as much alcohol. That means the effects of the alcohol stay in our bodies longer. Compared to men who drink, women have a greater risk of cirrhosis, liver disease, memory loss, and most frighteningly, shrinkage of the brain. Chronic alcohol use can also increase the risk of breast cancer and cancers of the mouth, throat, esophagus, liver, and colon.

Eleven

Motherhood May Not Be Enough

WHAT TO REALLY EXPECT:
It is possible to be both overwhelmed
and underwhelmed by the motherhood
experience at the same time.

Where did I go? I remember the first time I asked myself that question. I was invited to an alumni event at my alma mater Georgetown University. As a group of twenty or so former students sat around a table, we were asked to share what we were doing now. My heart started racing. What would I say? I had been laid off, so technically I was no longer an employed writer. I had always prided myself on my career. When my turn came up, I tentatively offered, "Well, I am a stay-at-home mom." Someone started clapping, then others joined in. The gesture, surely meant to lift me up, felt like mocking.

I looked around at the accomplished female alums (lawyer, entrepreneur, teachers, a Peace Corps volunteer) feeling as though I had let myself down. Was I proud to be a mom? Yes. It was the hardest thing I had ever done. To lean on that old cliché, motherhood is certainly the most important job out there. Who doesn't want to raise little humans that will someday turn into good people who lead wonderful lives, maybe even cure or invent something? But I didn't want that to be the only accomplishment that defined me. I wanted desperately to be something else as well.

This is not about having a particular career. That's not the antidote for everyone. You can go off to work every day and still feel this way. Being a mom has a way of overshadowing or even erasing everything we were before. So many women talked about an uneasiness they didn't anticipate. For them, being moms didn't complete them the way they thought it should. It's a revelation that comes with a great deal of guilt and shame. Motherhood should be enough, but what if it's not?

"There's this shift in identity, and I think that that can be hard to articulate immediately," explained therapist and author Esther Boykin, who sees this issue a great deal in her marriage and family practice. "It takes some time to really work through the question, 'Oh, who am I in the world now?' You developed who you are in the world as a woman and whatever other roles you've played. If you're married, you create your identity as a wife, and then you have a baby, and then there's a lot of pressure that that should somehow become not just your primary role but also the most important overarching theme of who you are in the world." What is important to understand is that this ambivalence is normal. It's all a part of your matrescence journey.

While the person you once were is still there, she's just been buried underneath the weight of your new life.

"I feel like I've lost parts of myself."

"I feel like I should be doing more."

"Is this all I am meant to be?"

"I have more to give than just being a mom."

How Did We Get Here?

The main issue here, again, is expectation—what we expect rarely matches the reality of the experience. We are told that nothing is more fulfilling than raising a family. And while that may be true, it's not always all that a woman needs to feel complete. The disillusionment happens in stages.

First there is the *waiting game*. You are well into your pregnancy, daydreaming about a maternity leave filled with free time. My own naïveté inspired me to plan on finishing that screenplay I had started a year earlier and to take up meditation while my baby napped. All ridiculous goals in hindsight. I had no idea that combing my hair would be a major accomplishment of the day. Other moms shared that they were sure they would spend their time "relaxing" with baby or sit curled up on the sofa watching her as she gurgled peacefully in that fancy swing someone gifted. One woman laughed remembering plans of nestling her infant daughter in a sling so "she could hear my heartbeat" during a sewing class, something she wanted to learn her entire life. Then she met her whirling dervish of a baby. She couldn't keep her in a carrier for more than five minutes. Forget an hour.

There is so much you are blissfully unaware of, and that is how it is for most new parents. It's harder than you ever imagined. To be fair, how can you really understand something like sleep deprivation until you are that breastfeeding zombie at a 4:00 a.m. feed? How can you understand the horror of cracked and bleeding nipples until you have cracked and bleeding nipples?

Then comes the *dazed and confused* portion of your existence. You get that it's hard, but now you understand that it will be this hard for a very long time. Everything has changed—your relationships, your body, and your will to live (just kidding). New patterns really start to take shape in your life. At one point you thought a child would fit into your world. Now you feel as though your life has to be reformed around your child's wants and needs. It's playdates, baby music classes, and doctor appointments. It's rushing out of work every day at 5:30 to pick up from daycare or relieve the nanny and then begin your second shift of making dinner, doing laundry, and getting the baby to bed. This is the new normal.

The last stage is what I like to call *the reckoning*. You take stock of your life. You are tired. You are overwhelmed. "Is this it?" many moms ask, ashamed the words even emerged from their lips. Sometimes there are tears because the store was out of your brand of diapers or because your baby won't sleep for more than twenty minutes at a time or because you haven't seen a friend in weeks. "Aren't I supposed to be more grateful than this? Isn't motherhood supposed to be enough?"

I am here to tell you that it's okay if it isn't. It doesn't mean that you don't love your child. It doesn't mean you don't cherish your family. What it means is that you need a little more in addition to that. A lot of women do.

Who You Are vs. Who You Want to Be

Sometimes, you are forced to confront this unexpectedly. Natalie, that mom of two from Connecticut first introduced at the beginning of the book, was working her dream job as a producer in California when she got pregnant. "I was in the career zone," she explained. Then her husband got a new job on the East Coast, and they had to move when she was thirty-six weeks along. "Everything I knew changed on a dime. I had sciatica. I was so big I could barely move. I wasn't sure what was going to happen to my career. What just happened to me? My whole adult life I had prided myself on my career. By choice, I put my child first, but that doesn't mean it was easy. It wasn't easy to let go of Natalie the career woman and become Natalie the mommy."

Her inner battle was clear: after her daughter was born, she didn't want to work 24/7 but she also didn't want to be a stay-at-home mom either. "I was grieving my former life," she added. "It took a toll on my mental health and outlook. I couldn't enjoy those early days because I was beating myself up because I couldn't have it all."

While she loved being a mom, she felt the need to prove she wasn't *just* a mom. She had to reconcile who she was and who she wanted to be. The solution became clear as she started writing about her experiences. She channeled her years of experience as a journalist into NatsNextAdventure .com where she writes about motherhood and mental health.

Her vulnerability and honesty have helped an untold number of mothers who silently share similar struggles.

This is hardest to accept for moms who are "baby crazy" from the start. Those women who babysat since junior high, dreamed of having families of their own for as long as they can remember, always knew children were in their future. They imagined spending long days with their future children, showing them the world, teaching them things. Then the child arrives, and it's nothing like they had hoped.

It's not just that it's hard. What really leaves so many women riddled with guilt, fear, and shame is that they don't feel like they think they should. This was, after all, a role they had longed for their whole lives. But raising a child can challenge everything you believed about yourself. "When you bring a human life into the world—which is the hardest job on the planet—it really makes you look at your own life and your own sense of who you are," explained therapist Mullin, who also conducts Bringing Home Baby workshops that help couples prepare for the changes in their lives and marriage. It's not uncommon for her to see women go into motherhood feeling that it will complete them—and then reality hits. Mothers typically suffer in silence, feeling ashamed of the disappointment.

Parenthood Has No Pause Button

This is about how we see ourselves in this world, what we want to contribute to the world beyond raising children. Having the singular identity of mother can feel like an incomplete story, like a novel missing the last three chapters. As important as the role is, it's not all of who we are or who we want to be. It doesn't help that we are living in an age of continuous parenting; it's the notion that we are on duty 24/7 for eighteen years and beyond. Thanks to a combination of helicopter-parenting, philosophy, and technology, we are constantly on top of our children. Baby monitors help us keep a watchful eye at all times. There are even gadgets that enable us to keep abreast of their breathing and heart rates while sleeping in their cribs. As they get older, we saddle them with devices that allow us to track their whereabouts. We are in constant contact with our children. We should ask, Is this really necessary? Not long ago, parents would go out to dinner and have no idea how the kids behaved with the babysitter until they arrived back home. Today, American moms spend twice as much time with their children as did mothers fifty years ago.[1] One thing that I have learned about my own needs is that my sanity requires time away from my family. Sometimes that is going for a run; in more indulgent moments, it is a girls' trip.

On a recent weekend getaway with three other moms, it was hard to deny that I was still "on." At least three times a day I was fielding calls, texts, and emails about schedules, snacks, homework, and discipline. We all were. This trip happened to coincide with the beginning of the coronavirus outbreak in the US, and I received one message with a long list of supplies I "should order online right away." I did it because if I didn't, I figured no one else would. Even as I write this, I am wondering why I didn't insist he just do it. Was it so inconceivable? I didn't even ask. I just lapsed into my prescribed role as so many of us do. And therein lies the continual problem for moms.

The simple fact is that most moms are rarely if ever off duty, and it's burning us out. The media loves to talk about how we need "me time," but does self-care really have an impact if we never address why women are so fraught? A 2018 survey by the now-defunct meal delivery service Munchery found that parents get just thirty-two minutes a day to themselves.[2] I would argue it's even less. My toddler waits outside the bathroom, slipping his fingers under the door until I emerge. If I forget to lock it, he barges right in, and I have an audience. In a short amount of time, we are supposed to recharge. Is it any wonder mothers feel completely overwhelmed? Is it any wonder we crave something for ourselves?

Feeling this way does not mean you don't adore your children. The solution isn't to cut ourselves off from them. What we need is to create and maintain something for ourselves. Moms need to be able to clock out once in a while in order to cultivate a life of our own. For many moms, this tug for more manifests when the kids get a little older and a lot less needy—a natural turn that can leave us feeling both abandoned and lost. "This can't be it for me, can it?" a friend once asked over coffee. She had stopped working when she became a mom, and her kids, now in grade school, didn't seem to want her around as much. She went on, "I just don't believe this is my only thing, my only purpose." She just didn't know where to begin.

This is such a common scenario. Aruna, a mother of four living in rural Monroe, Georgia, shared tearfully, "I'm trying to find my direction and place in this life. I don't know what to do with myself." For Aruna, not working had been the more financially sound decision for a long time. Her husband is a truck driver, constantly on the road. With four young children, childcare expenses would have far exceeded what she could earn. As her kids got older and the bills kept mounting, going back to work became a necessity not only for the family's survival but for her emotional well-being as well. She just didn't know how to make a change. She has a bachelor's degree in English but had no idea what she would be good at or what would make her happy. She considered medical billing, driving a school bus, or even teaching, but wondered, "Do I want to take on other people's kids when my own drive me nuts?"

Then there was the all-too-familiar complaint about her partner: he doesn't do nearly enough to help out. She knows that going back to work means carrying a full load inside and outside the house. "He will go and take a dump for an hour, and in that time, I've showered the kids, got them dressed, and packed the baby bag," she lamented. "By the time he's dressed, he's wondering why I am not finished yet. I just want to ask, 'Are you an asshole, or are you just looking for death?' Men can do so much more to take just an inch of the pressure off a wife or mother. It would go such a long way. If you see a sock on the floor, pick it up. It helps." Once in a blue moon, she says, he steps up, takes the reins with the kids to give her a couple hours to just breathe. But she craves so much more than that short break.

In the six months between our first conversation and this writing, much changed for Aruna. Her husband was placed on disability leave from his job, and they moved in with her in-laws. Things were scary, but she was driven and applied to be a detention center officer, with a longer-term goal of becoming a deputy sheriff. Scared but hopeful is the best way to describe her mood these days. For the first time in a long while, she has something new to look forward to. Something she feels is as much for her as it is for her family.

Finding Purpose Beyond Parenthood

Getting a new job or figuring out your dream career isn't the universal antidote, of course. About 43 percent of women with children leave the workforce voluntarily for a period of time.[3] Sometimes, like in the case of Aruna, the cost of childcare makes the decision to leave the workforce a practical one. I encountered many former lawyers, c-suite executives, and other once-high-powered women who happily gave up their careers for their children. Regardless, their savvy and acumen, once reserved for boardrooms, now helps them micromanage their families and take on leadership roles at their children's schools or at charitable organizations. Having more means something different to every woman. We tend to deprive ourselves of activities that feed the other part of who we are. This is about feeling less invisible and using that untapped potential. Consider it a sanity-saving haven.

It's natural to wonder how the hell you do this with all you have on your plate. How do you become the person you need and want to be? You have to start by giving yourself permission to seek out your passion and purpose. For some moms, it's about fitness, meditation, or advanced coursework or going to graduate school. I met women who carved out space to become yoga instructors, programmers, and chefs. Another got a degree in social work at nights. Others pursued stamp collecting, quilting, and kombucha brewing (which I didn't even realize was a thing). The point is not what you do but that you continue to center yourself, grow, and achieve things that make you happy.

The Joy of Giving Back

It's hard not to be awed by mothers like Terry, who started a charity while raising her four children in Taylor, Michigan. Her organization, Enchanted Makeovers, goes into shelters that serve women and redecorates the rooms to give them a more homey, comfortable feel. Her goal was a simple one: to help mitigate the shame and embarrassment a family on the streets can experience, a feeling she knows all too well. Growing up, her family lost their home and had to "couch surf" from relative to relative. "This is a circumstance, not their identity," added Terry, who is especially proud that Enchanted Makeovers is a part of first crucial step toward a new life.

There is a lot of stigma to being homeless, and Terry's efforts go a long way in making the situation a little more bearable. She also discovered an unexpected benefit. She is creating a village for women so desperately in need of one. A lot of the women that she encounters have no relationship with their own mothers. "So many don't even know how to take care of a family—they don't know how to be mothers," she mused sympathetically. "It's this whole lack of basic life skills. I think that we bring help in the most loving way. No one feels judged. That's it. It's not really rocket science. It's just how I grew up, how my mother raised me. That's what I want to bring to women and children and new mothers."

There are opportunities to combine your passion with making an income. Laurie, a North Carolina mother of four, wanted to create something for parents who, like her, wanted to raise morally grounded children. Her Fruit-Full Kids line of dishware each includes a Bible verse or character trait that is supposed to serve as a conversation starter during mealtimes. "I feel like I'm fulfilling my purpose," she said. "Isn't that what we all want?" Indeed, it is.

Sometimes we just need to reaffirm our decision to stay focused on whatever it is that brings us joy. Remember Gaye, the corporate lawyer who was all about career for much of her adult life? When she and her husband decided to have kids, she didn't take a step back, but others thought she should cut her hours, be home more. She wondered: *Was she letting her boys down? Would they hate her for it? Was she being selfish? Her job made her happy, but was she supposed to give it up?* She finally embraced her career focus after her oldest son asked, "Can boys be lawyers too, Mommy, because I want to be just like you."

Still, those doubts are a common concern among working moms. I myself made a conscious decision to take a step back professionally to be more available for my family. When I worked crazy hours, I always felt tremendously guilty. It came to a head for me one Sunday afternoon when I took my son to the park and he quickly found a playmate, as kids do. His new BFF, a little girl, suggested they play mommy and daddy. "I'll be mommy," Lex said excitedly. Then he proceeded to march around in what was supposed to be an imitation of me: "I have to work. I have to work. No time to play. I have to work."

Hearing this motivated me to leave my magazine job that kept me at the office until two in the morning some days and lean a bit more into motherhood. But that didn't mean quitting altogether. My first few months as a mother had already taught me that I needed a life outside the confines of my baby and apartment. I took a position with a more family-friendly work schedule and shifted my focus to writing about parenthood. It gave me a new sense of purpose. I loved it.

Make a New Plan

Our partners need to understand that we are adjusting to who we are now. They, too, need to be schooled on matrescence and that, for many women, this is a natural part of our evolution. As you endeavor to change the family dynamic, you may get resistance from those who rely on you day to day. Don't back down.

Just the mental load of motherhood can be over-whelming, and there is no rule that says you have to do it all. If your spouse expects you to be a supermom, it's time to have a tough talk. I've talked a lot about the fact that moms are typically the default parent, taking care of every domestic need. This is the first thing you need to address. Sit down and come up with a more equitable division of labor. You should also get the kids more involved in household chores. Even a four-year-old is capable of picking up their things, making beds, getting their own snacks from the cupboard, and clearing the table.

If childcare is a hurdle, research area daycare or sign up for the aftercare program at your child's school. You also want to take advantage of all the help that's offered. I never appreciated my mother-in-law more than when I needed help with the kids when I was on deadline trying to finish this book.

My point here is that there are things you can do to ease the tension you feel between parenthood and other dreams deferred. You may be torn between two desires: to expand your life beyond your kids and to give them the best care possible. It's important to remember that this doesn't have to be an either-or proposition. Before you were a mom, you were someone. That person is still there. It's about finding a balance that is fair to you. Your children can be your proudest accomplishment, but no one ever said they have to be your only one.

YOUR NEW TO-DO LIST

Sit down with a notepad and answer each of these questions. They will lay the groundwork for figuring out what you need to do to pursue your dreams. Keep in mind that bliss and fulfillment look different for every mom, for every person. Find *your* happy.

1. When you were a little girl, what did you want to be when you grew up?

2. What is your dream job?

3. Other than your children, what fulfills you?

4. What do you think you need to be happy?

5. If you never tried to reach your goal, how would you feel?

6. What do you think is holding you back?

7. What can you do to get closer to your goal?

8. What was your dream before you had children?

9. If you could divide up your day any way you wanted, what would it look like?

10. Name three things you do for you and only you.

11. What do you think is your purpose in your family? What is your purpose beyond your family life?

12. What made you most proud before you had kids?

13. What change do you want to see in your life?

14. How do you want your children to see you?

15. What part of yourself do you want to share with the world?

16. If you were guaranteed success, what would you try?

Put Yourself Out There

This isn't easy for everyone. If it's a career you seek, there are now job placement organizations, such as Après, that specifically target moms, offering part-time, flextime, and shared positions. You may fear rejection. A lot of moms feel as though they may not have the skills necessary to start a new venture, but motherhood is better training than you can imagine. A couple of years with kids and I guarantee you are a master multitasker, can micromanage difficult underlings, creatively problem solve, and have the patience of Job.

Would you let your children give up without even trying? Would you encourage them to quit just because things became difficult? Of course, you wouldn't. Apply those same parenting instincts to yourself.

- Confidence is key. Being a parent has taught you more than you realize. Working moms are more organized and often show superior leadership skills. Running a household requires accounting, managing, organizational skills, patience, and diplomacy. You can use these skills to get back into the job market or land a better position.

- Each week make small steps toward your goal. This could mean sitting down with a headhunter or job placement office, figuring out babysitting options, researching better opportunities at your current workplace, or even taking online classes. Change doesn't come overnight.

- Be willing to make sacrifices. Returning to work will mean you will not be as available to your family as they are used to. When the guilt trip starts—and it will—remember that you deserve happiness, and it's more than okay to have your needs met too.

Everything Worth Doing Is a Little Scary

This can feel like an overwhelming game plan, I know. You should expect some guilt initially. Anything that takes more time away from your family is always a difficult undertaking for a mom. A promotion could mean more hours at work. A return to the working world means not being around as much as you used to. Though once you start to let go of your old expectations about motherhood, you will feel a tremendous weight lifted from your shoulders.

Yes, in many ways this is about having individual goals. You need to consider what *you* want and what *you* need, but the benefits will go well beyond your own happiness. Ask yourself what kind mother you want your kids to have. What kind of mother do you want your daughters to see? You need to give attention to those parts of yourself that have been neglected under a misguided notion of what a good mother must do and what a good mother must give up.

The Double Standard We Can't Shake

Men simply don't face this dilemma. No one ever asks him if he's going back to work after his child is born. Yes, dads are judged (mostly by their partners, I bet), but by and large, they just don't feel the same pressure about their choice to pursue whatever career goals or pastimes they desire. One wintery day, I had lunch with a woman who complained that her husband was like a 1950s dad, a character flaw (her words, not mine) that didn't come out until after they had a child. They both had busy jobs with long hours mind you, but when they got home, all the childcare fell on her shoulders. Their baby was six months old, and her husband had only changed a handful of diapers because "I'm so bad at it," he would say.

On Saturdays, he still spent half the day golfing because it is how he decompressed after a stressful week. It's an entitlement many (not all) men feel, not because they are terrible people, but because they have been raised in a world deeply rooted in sexism and gendered divisions of labor. We've all witnessed a man being praised for taking his kids to the park. "What a good dad," friends, family, and strangers will say. No one bats an eye when a mom does it—for the 5,365th time. Do I get a pat on the back when I quickly squash a temper tantrum at a restaurant so we all can dine in peace? No. And I don't expect one. What I do expect is to carve out time and space for Ericka.

I asked my husband how partners can equal the parenting playing field. He thought for a few moments and said, "Doing more at home. Not waiting to be asked." If this were a test, he'd score an A+. It's what we want to hear. Now we need that way of thinking to actually become second nature. Partners, employers, the culture, women, and men all need to step up to make it possible for moms to have the full and balanced lives we deserve. The change starts by asking for or even demanding what we need. Though I would be lying if I said that was enough. We need a cultural shift in the workplace too, one that actually respects mothers as much as it pretends to. Right now, it still often feels like we are tolerated rather than embraced for what we can offer. At the bare minimum, we shouldn't be on the receiving end of eye rolls and smirks when we have to leave early to take care of a sick child. Effective change means generous maternity leave policies for all new parents, flexible schedules, the option to work remotely (when it's feasible), the elimination of the penalties we often face, and fair opportunities for advancement and promotion. It's what we deserve.

This process of finding yourself won't always be an easy one. With matrescence, there will inevitably be highs and lows, successes and failures, as you continue to grow. "This thing is expanding the hell out of you, and you are finally standing up for your invisibility," cheered Dr. Athan. "Greater, deeper selfhood." The goal is to know yourself, to continually advocate for your needs. We don't have to be subservient to our role as parents any more than our partners do. My greatest hope is that we can finally stop asking, Where did I go? because we are no longer lost.

PARENT RESOURCES

A short list of recommendations by moms for moms to inspire, offer solutions, and most importantly, make you feel less alone in the struggle that is new motherhood.

Must Reads

Brody, Lauren Smith. *The Fifth Trimester: The Working Moms Guide to Style, Sanity, and Success after Baby.* New York: Anchor Books, 2018.

Brown, Brené. *Daring Greatly: How the Courage to Be Vulnerable Transforms the Way We Live, Love, Parent, and Lead.* New York: Avery, 2012.

Dunn, Jancee. *How Not to Hate Your Husband after Kids.* New York: Little, Brown, 2018.

Gefsky, Jennifer, and Stacey Delo. *Your Turn: Careers, Kids, and Comebacks—a Working Mother's Guide.* New York: HarperCollins, 2019.

McKowen, Laura. *We Are the Luckiest: The Surprising Magic of a Sober Life.* Novato, CA: New World Library, 2020.

O'Connell, Meaghan. *And Now We Have Everything: On Motherhood Before I Was Ready.* New York: Back Bay Books, 2019.

Powers, Lindsay. *You Can't F*ck Up Your Kids: A Judgment-Free Guide to Stress-Free Parenting.* New York: Atria, 2020.

Rodsky, Eve. *Fair Play: A Game-Changing Solution for When You Have Too Much to Do (and More Life to Live).* New York: G. P. Putnam's Sons, 2019.

Senior, Jennifer. *All Joy and No Fun: The Paradox of Modern Parenthood.* New York: HarperCollins, 2015.

Coaching & Career Guidance

The Fifth Trimester, thefifthtrimester.com

The Après Group, apresgroup.com

Emotional Support

Happy with Baby, happywithbaby.com

Help for Your Family, helpforyourfamily.com

The Mindful Mommy, themindfulmommy.com

Therapy Is Not a Dirty Word, therapyisnotadirtyword.com

The Gottman Institute, gottman.com/parents

The Motherhood Center, themotherhoodcenter.com

Postpartum Support

The Seleni Institute, seleni.org

Postpartum International, postpartum.net

The Bloom Foundation, bloomfoundation.com

Sobriety Support

Sober Mommies, sobermommies.com

Laura McKowen, lauramckowen.com

Hip Sobriety, hipsobriety.com

Caregivers

Care, care.com

Sitter City, sittercity.com

Urban Sitter, urbansitter.com

Au Pair Care, aupaircare.com

Podcasts

Motherhood Sessions

What Fresh Hell: Laughing in the Face of Motherhood

The Longest Shortest Time

Moms Don't Have Time to Read with Zibby Owens

ACKNOWLEDGMENTS

It's so cliché to say, but writing your first book is really a lot like giving birth. It's a process of growing and nurturing something that you put out into the world and hope it will do some good and somehow make things better. I could not have done that without a special group of people, a writer's village, if you will.

Thank you to my incredibly thoughtful editor Caroline Pincus at Sounds True, who guided me with brilliance and grace. You helped me craft a beautiful and honest message to moms. Thank you to my funny, frank, and engaging agent Jacqueline Flynn at the Joelle Delbourgo Agency for believing in this project from the start. Tossing ideas back and forth with you was one of the most enjoyable parts of this process. I am also grateful for my production editor Jade Lascelles, marketing manager Christine Day, publicity director Wendy Gardner, cover designer Jennifer Miles, and the entire Sounds True team, who made my first publishing experience so incredible. You magically turned these beloved pages into an actual book.

I would not have accomplished anything without wonderful mentors along the way. I wish every budding writer was lucky enough to have professors like I had at Georgetown University. Mary Esselman and Elizabeth Velez saw something in me I didn't know was there. It was with their encouragement that I pursued journalism.

And thank you to Professor Pamela Fox who taught me how to think critically, question, and create.

A special thanks to Garry Clifford who gave me my start as a reporting intern. You saw a curious and tenacious kid and, along with your team of stalwart reporters at the DC Bureau of *People* magazine, you molded me into a journalist. Thank you to Amy Boshnack, for hiring me as an editor at CafeMom, helping me transition from celebrity news to the ever-more fulfilling parenting realm. I learned so much under your savvy and wise direction.

To my girls: Sona Charaipotra, thank you for being the ultimate motivator and cheerleader. You have the biggest heart of anyone I know. Anika Awai Williams, you are my oldest, dearest friend. Never has there been a better confidante and partner in crime. Laura J. Downey, thank you for being my spiritual barometer and the one I can reach out to for a laugh even at two in the morning. Michelle West, Fen Yee Teh, and Robbie Bantom, you are the best college roomies of all time. We've grown up together and shared many laughs and life milestones. I am grateful to call you all dear friends.

Thank you Denise Courter, Diane Belan, Dawn Krigstin, Judy McCool, Monique Shottes, and the other moms of 80 John. You were among my first mom friends and made me realize that no, I wasn't the only one feeling completely out of her depth.

I owe an enormous debt of gratitude to my mom squad: Andrea Costa, Andrea Dubois, Anita Lahey, Bianca Jebbia, Bita Javadizadeh, Brooke Rhind, Christy Searl, Ella Georgiades, Frances Impellizzeri, Irene Anschlowar,

Michelle Bea, Rachel Roberge, Annie Small, Sali Shibilo, Sheila Latimer, and Tamecca Seril. You are the women who are there for me at every turn as we raise our children in this crazy city together. We celebrate each other, console each other, we love each other. I am not exaggerating when I say I couldn't do this without you.

Thank you to the incredible mom role models I have known throughout my life, all of whom taught me a different yet profound perspective on motherhood: So Sun Kim, Gwen Awai, Roxana Reed, Bianca Lyder, Nancy Crump, Stephanie Mayfield Gibson, Alicia Cain Moore, Dasha Smith, pastor Pearl Wilson, Ines Carrington, and my mother-in-law Linet Pitters. Kisha Johnson and Zoila Orellana, thank you for helping me care for my children so that I could have a career.

I am who I am because of the people who raised me. To my mom, Anita Smith, never has there been a more fierce and loving protector. Though my father, Eric Sóuter, is no longer with us, his attentive, caring spirit still guides me. When I was a young child, I was lucky enough to spend every day after school with my grandparents Richard and Ethel Smith. They taught me the immense value of family and family time. To my aunts Annie, Debbie, and Nancy Smith, thank you for your unconditional love and unwavering faith in me.

To my boys, Lex and Aidan, I love you more than you will ever know. Having a family to come home to at the end of every day gives me so much joy. And my sweet husband, Caleb, who always encourages and supports me. Thank you. I love you.

NOTES

Introduction

1. Adrienne Rich, *Of Woman Born: Motherhood as Experience and Institution* (New York: W. W. Norton , 1986), 35.

Chapter One:
The Myth of Modern Motherhood

1. Jennifer Glass, Robin W. Simon, and Matthew A. Andersson, "Parenthood and Happiness: Effects of Work-Family Reconciliation Policies in 22 OECD Countries," *AJS* 122, no. 3 (November 2016): 886–929, ncbi.nlm.nih.gov/pmc/articles/PMC5222535/pdf/nihms777984.pdf.

2. Pew Research Center, *Parenting in America: Outlook, Worries, Aspirations Are Strongly Linked to Financial Situation*, December 17, 2005, pewsocialtrends.org/2015/12/17/2-satisfaction-time-and-support/.

3. Rachel Margolis and Mikko Myrskylä, "Parental Well-Being Surrounding First Birth as a Determinant of Further Parity Progression," *Demography* 52 (2015): 1147–66, doi.org/10.1007/s13524-015-0413-2.

4. Lydia Maria Child, *The Mother's Book* (Boston: Carter, Hendee, and Babcock, 1831), 146.

5. Betty Friedan, *The Feminine Mystique* (New York: W. W. Norton, 1963).

6. Diane Negra and Yvonne Tasker, eds., "Introduction: Gender and Recessionary Culture," in *Gendering the Recession: Media and Culture in an Age of Austerity* (Durham, NC: Duke University Press, 2014).

7. Pew Research Center, *Parenting in America*.

8. Philip Cowan, Carolyn Cowan, and Neera Mehta, "Adult Attachment, Couple Attachment, and Children's Adaptation to School: An Integrated Attachment Template and Family Risk Model," *Attachment & Human Development* 11 (February 2009): 29–46, researchgate.net/publication/23984008.

9. Cowan, Cowan, and Mehta, "Adult Attachment, Couple Attachment, and Children's Adaptation to School."

10. Christine Carter, *Raising Happiness: 10 Simple Steps for More Joyful Kids and Happier Parents* (New York: Ballantine Books, 2011), 5–7.

11. Nina Richter, Rebecca Bondü, C. Katharina Spiess, Gert G. Wagner, and Gisela Trommsdorff, "Relations Among Maternal Life Satisfaction, Shared Activities, and Child Well-Being," *Frontiers in Psychology* 9 (2018): 739, doi.org/10.3389/fpsyg.2018.00739.

Chapter Two:
The Motherhood Penalty

1. Linda Dwoskin and Rhiannon DiClemente, "INSIGHT: What to Expect When Your Employees Are Pregnant or New Parents," Daily Labor Report,

Bloomberg Law, December 3, 2018, news.bloomberglaw.com/daily-labor-report /insight-what-to-expect-when-your-employees-are -pregnant-or-new-parents.

2. Bureau of Labor Statistics National Compensation Survey, www.bls.gov/ncs/ebs/factsheet/family-leave -benefits-fact-sheet.htm.

3. Helene Jorgensen and Eileen Applebaum, "Expanding Federal Family and Medical Leave Coverage," Center for Economic and Policy Research (February 2014), cepr.net/documents/fmla-eligibility-2014-01.pdf.

4. Joan C. Williams and Nancy Segal, "Beyond the Maternal Wall: Relief for Family Caregivers Who Are Discriminated Against on the Job," *Harvard Women's Law Journal* 26, (2003): 77, repository .uchastings.edu/faculty_scholarship/805.

5. Caroline Fairchild, "Nearly Half of Mothers Work, Take a Break, and Work Again. Why Is There Still Such a Stigma?" LinkedIn, March 4, 2020, linkedin .com/pulse/nearly-half-mothers-work-take-break -again-why-still-stigma-fairchild/.

6. Madeline Heilman and Tyler Okimoto, "Motherhood: A Potential Source of Bias in Employment Decisions," *Journal of Applied Psychology* 93 (February 2008): 189–98, researchgate.net/publication/5640901 _Motherhood_A_Potential_Source_of_Bias_in _Employment_Decisions.

7. Michelle J. Budig, "The Fatherhood Bonus and the Motherhood Penalty: Parenthood and the Gender Gap in Pay," Third Way, September 2, 2014, thirdway.org /report/the-fatherhood-bonus-and-the-motherhood -penalty-parenthood-and-the-gender-gap-in-pay.

8. Budig, "Fatherhood Bonus and the Motherhood Penalty."

9. Kayla Patrick and Jasmine Tucker, "Equal Pay for Mothers Is Critical for Families," National Women's Law Center, May 2018, nwlc.org/resources /equal-pay-for-mothers-is-critical-for-families/.

10. Shelley J. Correll, Stephen Benard, and In Paik, "Getting a Job: Is There a Motherhood Penalty," *American Journal of Sociology* 112 (March 2007): 1297–1338, sociology.stanford.edu/sites/g/files /sbiybj9501/f/publications/getting_a_job-_is _there_a_motherhood_penalty.pdf.

11. Katharine Zaleski, "Female Company President: 'I'm Sorry to All the Mothers I Worked With,'" *Fortune*, March 3, 2015, fortune.com/2015/03/03 /female-company-president-im-sorry-to-all-the-mothers -i-used-to-work-with/.

12. Cynthia Thomas Calvert, "Caregivers in the Workplace: Family Responsibilities Discrimination Litigation Update 2016," Center for WorkLife Law, 13–14, worklifelaw.org/publications/Caregivers -in-the-Workplace-FRD-update-2016.pdf.

13. Bright Horizons, "Modern Family Index 2018," brighthorizons.com/-/media/BH-New/Newsroom/Media-Kit/MFI_2018_Report_FINAL.ashx.

14. Bright Horizons, "Modern Family Index 2018."

15. Matthias Krapf, Heinrich W. Ursprung, and Christian Zimmermann, "Parenthood and Productivity of Highly Skilled Labor: Evidence from the Groves of Academe," Federal Reserve Bank of St. Louis, Research Division Working Paper Series, January 2014, s3.amazonaws.com/real.stlouisfed.org/wp/2014/2014-001.pdf.

16. Joan C. Williams and Amy J. C. Cuddy, "Will Working Mothers Take Your Company to Court?" *Harvard Business Review*, September 2012, hbr.org/2012/09/will-working-mothers-take-your-company-to-court.

17. Save the Children, "Nutrition in the First 1,000 Days," State of the World's Mothers 2012, May 2012, savethechildren.org/content/dam/usa/reports/advocacy/sowm/sowm-2012.pdf.

Chapter Three:
It Takes a Village . . . for You

1. The Cigna US Loneliness Index is based on the UCLA Loneliness Scale, a twenty-item questionnaire developed to assess subjective feelings of loneliness or social isolation. The UCLA Loneliness Scale is a frequently referenced and acknowledged academic measure used to gauge loneliness. Respondents were

assigned a loneliness score based on their responses, with higher scores indicating increased loneliness. Approximately 20,096 adults ages eighteen and over from the continental US, Alaska, and Hawaii were surveyed online by IpsosPolling. Cigna, "Cigna US Loneliness Index," 2018, cigna.com/assets/docs /newsroom/loneliness-survey-2018-full-report.pdf.

2. Cigna, "Cigna US Loneliness Index."

3. Ning Xia and Huige Li, "Loneliness, Social Isolation, and Cardiovascular Health," *Antioxid Redox Signal* 28, no. 9 (2018): 837–51, doi:10.1089/ars.2017.7312.

4. Henri Nouwen, *Discernment: Reading the Signs of Daily Life* (New York: HarperOne, 2013).

5. Jeffrey Hall, "How Many Hours Does It Take to Make a Friend?" *Journal of Social and Personal Relationships* 36, no. 4 (2018): 1, journals.sagepub .com/doi/full/10.1177/0265407518761225.

6. Eun K. Shin, Kaja LeWinn, Nicole Bush, Frances A. Tylavsky, Robert L. Davis, and Arash Shaban-Nejad, "Association of Maternal Social Relationships with Cognitive Development in Early Childhood," *JAMA Network Open* 2, no. 1 (January 11, 2019): e186963, doi:10.1001/jamanetworkopen.2018.6963.

Chapter Four:
The Real Mommy War

1. Jan Jarboe Russell, "The Mommy War," *Texas Monthly*, July 1989.

2. Page Evans, "Sharks and Jets," in *Mommy Wars: Stay-at-Home and Career Moms Face Off on Their Choices, Their Lives, Their Families*, ed. Leslie Morgan Steiner (New York: Random House, 2006), 46.

3. Mark DeWolf, "12 Stats about Working Women," US Department of Labor, March 1, 2017, blog.dol.gov/2017/03/01/12-stats-about-working-women.

4. C.S. Mott Children's Hospital, "Mom Shaming or Constructive Criticism? Perspectives of Mothers," National Poll on Children's Health, *Mott Poll Report*, 29, no. 3 (June 19, 2017), mottpoll.org/sites/default/files/documents/061917_criticizingmoms.pdf.

5. Leora Tanenbaum, *Catfight: Women and Competition* (New York: Seven Stories Press, 2002), 15.

6. Susan Douglas and Meredith Michaels, *The Mommy Myth: The Idealization of Motherhood and How It Has Undermined Women* (New York: Free Press, 2004), 6.

7. Phyllis Chesler, *Woman's Inhumanity to Woman* (Chicago: Lawrence Hill Books, 2009), 2.

Chapter Five:
No Kidding

1. Leslie Ashburn-Nardo, "Parenthood as a Moral Imperative? Moral Outrage and the Stigmatization of Voluntarily Childfree Women and Men," *Sex Roles* 76 (2017): 393–401, doi.org/10.1007/s11199-016-0606-1.

2. Pew Research Center, "America's Changing Religious Landscape," May 12, 2005, pewforum.org/2015/05/12/americas-changing-religious-landscape/.

3. Scott Neuman, "Couples Who Choose Not to Have Children Are 'Selfish,' Pope Says," NPR, February 12, 2015, npr.org/sections/thetwo-way/2015/02/12/385735269/couples-who-chose-not-to-have-children-are-selfish-pope-says.

4. Leta S. Hollingworth, "Social Devices for Impelling Women to Bear and Rear Children," *American Journal of Sociology* 22, no. 1 (July 1916): 19–29, jstor.org/stable/2763926?seq=4#metadata_info_tab_contents.

5. Hollingworth, "Social Devices for Impelling Women to Bear and Rear Children."

6. Hollingworth, "Social Devices for Impelling Women to Bear and Rear Children."

7. Laura Carroll, *The Baby Matrix: Why Freeing Our Minds from Outmoded Thinking about Parenthood & Reproduction Will Create a Better World* (LiveTrue Books, 2012), 15.

8. Ellen Peck, *The Baby Trap* (New York: Pinnacle Books, 1971), 184.

9. Peck, *The Baby Trap*, 186.

10. Peck, *The Baby Trap*, 187.

11. Jacqui Gabb, Martina Klett-Davies, Janet Fink, and Manuela Thomae, "Enduring Love? Couple Relationships in the 21st Century," Survey Findings

Report, The Open University (2013): 24, open.ac.uk
/researchprojects/enduringlove/sites/www.open.ac.uk
.researchprojects.enduringlove/files/files/ecms/web
-content/Final-Enduring-Love-Survey-Report.pdf.

12. Gary J. Gates, "Marriage and Family: LGBT
Individuals and Same-Sex Couples," *Future of
Children* 25, no. 2 (2015): 72, files.eric.ed.gov/fulltext
/EJ1079373.pdf; Equal Family Council, LGBTQ
Factsheet, www2.census.gov/cac/nac/meetings
/2017-11/LGBTQ-families-factsheet.pdf.

13. Victoria Clarke, Nikki Hayfield, Sonja Ellis, and
Gareth Terry, "Lived Experiences of Childfree
Lesbians in the United Kingdom: A Qualitative
Exploration," *Journal of Family Issues* 39 (December
2018): 4133–55, researchgate.net/publication
/328856086_Lived_Experiences_of_Childfree
_Lesbians_in_the_United_Kingdom_A
_Qualitative_Exploration.

14. Satoshi Kanazawa, *The Intelligence Paradox: Why the
Intelligent Choice Isn't Always the Smart One* (Hoboken,
NJ: John Wiley & Sons, 2012), 181.

15. Gretchen Livingston and D'Vera Cohn, "Childlessness
Up Among All Women; Down Among Women with
Advanced Degrees," June 25, 2010, pewsocialtrends
.org/2010/06/25/childlessness-up-among-all-women
-down-among-women-with-advanced-degrees/.

Chapter Six:
Post-Kid Marriage

1. Thomas Hansen, "Parenthood and Happiness: A Review of Folk Theories Versus Empirical Evidence," *Social Indicators Research* 108 (August 2012): 29–64, doi.org/10.1007/s11205-011-9865-y.

2. Gretchen Livingston, "Stay-at-Home Moms and Dads Account for about One-in-Five US Parents," Pew Research Center, September 24, 2018, pewresearch .org/fact-tank/2018/09/24/stay-at-home-moms-and -dads-account-for-about-one-in-five-u-s-parents/.

3. UN Women, "Turning Promises into Action: Gender Equality in the 2030 Agenda for Sustainable Development," United Nations report, 2018, unwomen.org/-/media/headquarters/attachments /sections/library/publications/2018/sdg-report-summary -gender-equality-in-the-2030-agenda-for-sustainable -development-2018-en.pdf?la=en&vs=949.

4. Olivia Remes, Carol Brayne, Rianne van der Linde, and Louise Lafortune, "A Systematic Review of Reviews on the Prevalence of Anxiety Disorders in Adult Populations," *Brain and Behavior* 6, no. 7 (July 2017): e00497.

5. Lucia Ciciolla and Suniya Luthar, "Invisible Household Labor and Ramifications for Adjustment: Mothers as Captains of Households," *Sex Roles* (January 2019): 1–20, researchgate.net/publication/330847401_Invisible _Household_Labor_and_Ramifications_for_Adjustment _Mothers_as_Captains_of_Households.

6. Alyson F. Shapiro, John M. Gottman, and Brandi C. Fink, "Short-Term Change in Couples' Conflict Following a Transition to Parenthood Intervention," *Couple and Family Psychology* 4, no. 4 (2015): 239–51, doi:10.1037/cfp0000051.

Chapter Seven:
Who Needs the "I Have a Headache" Excuse When You Have Kids?

1. Mattress company Leesa surveyed 977 parents to gauge how their sex lives changed after they added to their family. Leesa, "Your Sex Life After Having Kids: Exploring Intimacy Changes After Having Children," leesa.com/pages/parents-and-sex.

2. James Davis, "Age, Birth Cohort, Monotony, and Sex Frequency Among US Adults in the NORC General Social Surveys 1989–2000," April 2003, gss.norc.org /Documents/reports/topical-reports/TR36.pdf.

3. Kathleen Deveny, "We're Not in the Mood," *Newsweek*, June 2003, newsweek.com/were-not-mood-138387.

4. Leesa, "Your Sex Life After Having Kids."

5. Centers for Disease Control and Prevention, "Pregnancy-Related Deaths," cdc.gov/reproductivehealth /maternalinfanthealth/pregnancy-relatedmortality.htm; Centers for Disease Control and Prevention, "Pregnancy Complications," cdc.gov/reproductivehealth /maternalinfanthealth/pregnancy-complications.html.

6. Common Sense Media, "Children, Teens, Media and Body Image: A Common Sense Research Brief," January 21, 2015, commonsensemedia.org/research /children-teens-media-and-body-image.

7. Cynthia A. Graham, Catherine H. Mercer, Clare Tanton, Kyle G. Jones, Anne M. Johnson, Kaye Wellings, and Kirstin R. Mitchell, "What Factors Are Associated with Reporting Lacking Interest in Sex and How Do These Vary by Gender? Findings from the Third British National Survey of Sexual Attitudes and Lifestyles," *BMJ Open* 7, no. 9 (2017): e016942, doi:10.1136/bmjopen-2017-016942.

8. E. Mark Cummings, Melissa R. W. George, Kathleen P. McCoy, and Patrick T. Davies, "Interparental Conflict in Kindergarten and Adolescent Adjustment: Prospective Investigation of Emotional Security as an Explanatory Mechanism," *Child Development* 83, no. 5, (September/October 2012): 1703–15, doi .org/10.1111/j.1467-8624.2012.01807.x.

9. Lynn K. White and Alan Booth, "The Transition to Parenthood and Marital Quality," *Journal of Family Issues* 6, no. 4 (December 1, 1985): 435–49, journals .sagepub.com/doi/10.1177/019251385006004003.

10. Stephanie L. McFall and Chris Garrington, eds., *Early Findings from the First Wave of the UK's Household Longitudinal Study* (Colchester, UK: Institute for Social and Economic Research, University of Essex,

2011), repository.essex.ac.uk/9115/1
/Understanding-Society-Early-Findings.pdf.

11. Ayelet Waldman, "Truly, Madly, Guiltily," Modern
Love, *New York Times*, March 27, 2005, nytimes.com
/2005/03/27/fashion/truly-madly-guiltily.html.

12. Us Weekly Staff, "Giuliana Rancic: 'We Put Our
Marriage First and Our Child Second,'" *Us Weekly*,
February 27, 2013, usmagazine.com/celebrity
-moms/news/giuliana-rancic-we-put-our-marriage
-first-and-our-child-second-2013272/.

13. Hana Yoo, Suzanne Bartle-Haring, Randal D. Day,
and Rashmi Gangamma, "Couple Communication,
Emotional and Sexual Intimacy, and Relationship
Satisfaction," *Journal of Sex and Marital Therapy* 40, no. 4
(2014): 275–93, ncbi.nlm.nih.gov/pubmed/24111536.

Chapter Eight:
Not Every Woman Has the Mom Gene

1. Jennifer R. Brown, Hong Ye, and Roderick T. Bronson,
"A Defect in Nurturing in Mice Lacking the Immediate
Early Gene *fosB*," *Cell* 86 (July 26, 1996): 297–309,
doi.org/10.1016/S0092-8674(00)80101-4.

2. Wolf Reik and Jörn Walter, "Genomic Imprinting:
Parental Influence on the Genome," *Nature Reviews
Genetics* 2 (2001): 21–32, doi.org/10.1038/35047554.

3. Kris Y. W. Lok, Charlotte L. Y. Chow, Heidi S.
L. Fan, Vincci H. S. Chan, and Marie Tarrant,

"Exposure to Baby-Friendly Hospital Practices and Mothers' Achievement of Their Planned Duration of Breastfeeding," *BMC Pregnancy Childbirth* 20, no. 1 (May 1, 2020): 261, doi:10.1186/s12884-020-02904-0.

4. ITV, "Meghan Admits She Was 'Naïve' about British Tabloids and Reveals She Was Warned 'They Will Destroy Your Life,'" October 20, 2019, itv.com /news/2019-10-20/harry-and-meghan -an-african-journey.

5. Narasimhaiah G. Manjunath, Giriyappa Venkatesh, and Rajanna, "Postpartum Blue Is Common in Socially and Economically Insecure Mothers," *Indian Journal of Community Medicine* 36, no. 3 (July–September 2011): 231–33, ncbi.nlm.nih .gov/pmc/articles/PMC3214451/.

6. Postpartum Support International, "Depression During Pregnancy & Postpartum," postpartum.net /learn-more/depression-during-pregnancy-postpartum/.

7. Postpartum Support International, "Anxiety During Pregnancy & Postpartum," postpartum.net/learn-more /anxiety-during-pregnancy-postpartum/.

8. Postpartum Support International, "Pregnancy or Postpartum Obsessive Symptoms," postpartum.net /learn-more/pregnancy-or-postpartum -obsessive-symptoms/.

9. Postpartum Support International, "Postpartum Psychosis," postpartum.net/learn-more /postpartum-psychosis/.

Chapter Nine:
The Single-Minded

1. Timothy Grall, *Custodial Mothers and Fathers and Their Child Support: 2015*, US Census Bureau, May 2020, www2.census.gov/programs-surveys/demo /tables/families/2015/chldsu15.pdf.

2. Gretchen Livingston, "About One-Third of US Children Are Living with an Unmmaried Parent," Pew Research Center, April 27, 2018, pewresearch .org/fact-tank/2018/04/27/about-one-third-of-u-s -children-are-living-with-an-unmarried-parent/; Gretchen Livingston, "The Changing Profile of Unmarried Parents," Pew Research Center, April 25, 2018, pewsocialtrends.org/2018/04/25 /the-changing-profile-of-unmarried-parents/; Eli Rapoport, Nallammai Muthiah, Sarah A. Keim, and Andrew Adesman, "Family Well-Being in Grandparent-Versus Parent-Headed Households," *Pediatrics* 46, no. 3 (2020), pediatrics.aappublications .org/content/pediatrics/146/3/e20200115.full.pdf; Claire Cain Miller, "Americans Are Having Fewer Babies, They Told Us Why," *New York Times*, July 5, 2018, nytimes.com/2018/07/05/upshot /americans-are-having-fewer-babies-they-told-us -why.html.

3. European Society of Human Reproduction and Embryology, "Children in Single-Mother-by-Choice Families Do Just as Well as Those in Two-Parent Families: Family Social Support

Services Are Valued," *ScienceDaily*, July 5, 2017, sciencedaily.com/releases/2017/07 /170705095332.htm.

4. Livingston, "Changing Profile of Unmarried Parents."

Chapter Ten:
It's Mommy's Turn to Wine

1. Megan E. Slater, Sarah P. Haughwout, I-Jen P. Castle, "Trends in Substance Use Among Reproductive-Age Females in the United States, 2002–2013," National Institute on Alcohol Abuse and Alcoholism, September 2015, pubs.niaaa.nih .gov/publications/surveillance103/subst01.htm.

2. Bridget F. Grant, S. Patricia Chou, Tulshi D. Saha, Roger P. Pickering, Bradley T. Kerridge, W. June Ruan, Boji Huang, et al., "Prevalence of 12-Month Alcohol Use, High-Risk Drinking, and *DSM-IV* Alcohol Use Disorder in the United States, 2001–2002 to 2012– 2013: Results from the National Epidemiologic Survey on Alcohol and Related Conditions," *JAMA Psychiatry* 74, no. 9 (2017): 911–23, doi:10.1001/ jamapsychiatry.2017.2161.

3. Sarah A. Benton, "Caron Study Reveals 'Top 5 Reasons' Mothers Turn to Alcohol," Psychology Today, May 10, 2013, psychologytoday.com/us /blog/the-high-functioning-alcoholic/201305/caron -study-reveals-top-5-reasons-mothers-turn-alcohol.

4. Lawrence K. Altman, "Valium, Most Prescribed Drug, Is Center of Medical Dispute," *New York Times*, May 19, 1974, nytimes.com/1974/05/19/archives/valium-most-prescribed-drug-is-center-of-a-medical-dispute-wide-use.html.

5. FDA complete summary of Valium that includes clinical pharmacology, uses and risk factors, accessdata.fda.gov/drugsatfda_docs/label/2016/013263s094lbl.pdf.

Chapter Eleven:
Motherhood May Not Be Enough

1. Giulia M. Dotti Sani and Judith Treas, "Educational Gradients in Parents' Child-Care Time Across Countries, 1965–2012," *Family Relations* 78 (April 19, 2016): 1083–96, doi.org/10.1111/jomf.12305.

2. Tyler Schmall, "Parents Never Get Any Alone Time, Study Finds," SWNS Digital, October 3, 2018, swnsdigital.com/2018/10/parents-never-get-any-alone-time-study-finds/.

3. Sylvia Ann Hewlett and Carolyn Buck Luce, "Off-Ramps and On-Ramps: Keeping Talented Women on the Road to Success," *Harvard Business Review* 83, no. 3 (2005): 44, hbr.org/2005/03/off-ramps-and-on-ramps-keeping-talented-women-on-the-road-to-success.

ABOUT THE AUTHOR

Ericka Sóuter has more than twenty years of journalism experience and is a nationally recognized voice in parenting news and parenting advice. A frequent contributor on *Good Morning America* and other national broadcast outlets, it's her job to speak to parents across the country and to stay on top of the issues, controversies, and trends most affecting families today. Her work appears on the Bump, What to Expect, CafeMom, and Mom.com, all high-traffic parenting sites that reach millions of moms each month. Her writing has also been featured in *People* magazine, *Us Weekly*, *Essence*, *Cosmopolitan*, *Self*, and WebMD. Ericka received her bachelor's degree from Georgetown University and a master's degree from the Columbia University Graduate School of Journalism. A native of Ann Arbor, Michigan, she currently lives in New York City with her husband, Caleb, and her sons, Lex and Aidan.

ABOUT SOUNDS TRUE

Sounds True is a multimedia publisher whose mission is to inspire and support personal transformation and spiritual awakening. Founded in 1985 and located in Boulder, Colorado, we work with many of the leading spiritual teachers, thinkers, healers, and visionary artists of our time. We strive with every title to preserve the essential "living wisdom" of the author or artist. It is our goal to create products that not only provide information to a reader or listener but also embody the quality of a wisdom transmission.

For those seeking genuine transformation, Sounds True is your trusted partner. At SoundsTrue.com you will find a wealth of free resources to support your journey, including exclusive weekly audio interviews, free downloads, interactive learning tools, and other special savings on all our titles.

To learn more, please visit SoundsTrue.com/freegifts or call us toll-free at 800.333.9185.